SACRED LAMP AT DUSK

POEMS OF EDASSERI TRANSLATED INTO ENGLISH

ASOKAKUMAR EDASSERI

Copyright © ASOKAKUMAR EDASSERI
All Rights Reserved.

This book has been self-published with all reasonable efforts taken to make the material error-free by the author. No part of this book shall be used, reproduced in any manner whatsoever without written permission from the author, except in the case of brief quotations embodied in critical articles and reviews.

The Author of this book is solely responsible and liable for its content including but not limited to the views, representations, descriptions, statements, information, opinions and references ["Content"]. The Content of this book shall not constitute or be construed or deemed to reflect the opinion or expression of the Publisher or Editor. Neither the Publisher nor Editor endorse or approve the Content of this book or guarantee the reliability, accuracy or completeness of the Content published herein and do not make any representations or warranties of any kind, express or implied, including but not limited to the implied warranties of merchantability, fitness for a particular purpose. The Publisher and Editor shall not be liable whatsoever for any errors, omissions, whether such errors or omissions result from negligence, accident, or any other cause or claims for loss or damages of any kind, including without limitation, indirect or consequential loss or damage arising out of use, inability to use, or about the reliability, accuracy or sufficiency of the information contained in this book.

Made with ♥ on the Notion Press Platform
www.notionpress.com

This book is dedicated to my mother (late) E. Janaki Amma, wife of the poet, (late) Edasseri Govindan Nair.

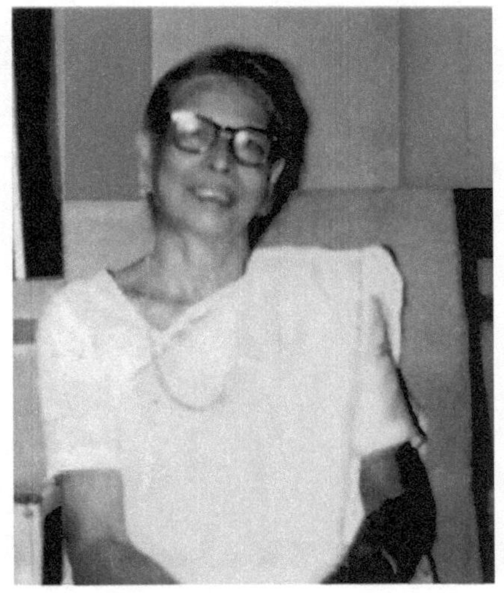

E. Janaki Amma (26.03.1916 – 27.09.1988)

Contents

Foreword

EDASSERI - THE VIRAAT PURUSHA

K. V. Ramakrishnan

Mahakavi Edasseri once appeared before me as the All-Pervading, the Ubiquitous Force, expanding itself, germinating all the three worlds - the Paathaalam (Hades), the Bhoomi (Earth), and the Swargam (Heaven) - as the Viraat Purusha. It was while standing on the northern bank, across Ponani, of the flooded Bhaarathappuzha, listening to the roaring waves of the not-too-far-away sea, Edasseri said:

"My kin, there is no going back
Without taking you across."
And then,
"A moment - there stands Edasseri in the bottomless depths
Deeper than the waves, the river, and the sea;
A moment - there stands Edasseri on the heights
Higher than the galaxy."
(Remembering Edasseri - Vishnunarayanan Namboodiri)

And, as I stand bewildered, winking and winking, there stands Edasseri, now a child all dressed up by the elder sister, ready to be taken to school for the first time. He is in front of his father, seeking the father's blessings on this auspicious occasion.

Father who aged; his words never faltering
Gave his son this blessing, rather this order;

Learn to write neatly!
So unmindful was he, when
He moulded that beautiful concept;
Whether a bush of thorny shrubs,
Or a bed of jasmine flowers!
He was only suggesting
An unfettered straight path.
That concept was good; And
I bow myself at his sacred feet
For, my burdensome days traverse
Along that hard path even today!
('To School, Again' - Edasseri)

Walking along that rough road of 'handwriting' - of 'words' – 'words' of poems and of documents, he reached the maturity of the solemn philosophy:

'Whatever you want to be, you be;
Let that bud bloom from within.
You have a secured heart
And a healthy tender body.
What I wish for you is this;
Even after gaining abundance of knowledge,
Let it remain unceasingly in you;
The brilliance of mind and a healthy body!'
('To School, Again' - Edasseri)

Now, in front of the great poet was standing his own child, all dressed up by the elder sister, ready to be taken to school for the first time, seeking the father's blessings!

Here is a Man! One, who walked along the rough road of his full life, imbibing the spirit from his father, 'who grew old walking with unfaltering words'.

'I cherish riding this chariot
Along this uneven road;
Let this roll through any dark hole,
I won't leave these rays.'
(Again to Ambaadi - Edasseri)

One, who walked with unfaltering steps along the rough road covered with cluster of thorns. 'Steps' are 'padangal' in Malayalam language - meaning 'words and feet' too! Remember, the word the poet uses in the above stanza is 'rasmikal' which means 'rays' and 'reins' as well.

'I am sitting at my writing desk,
And now, my room is over-crowded.
They want their documents written;
I prefer writing poems.'
(Elopement - Edasseri)

This is a daily routine. And, in this eternal flow of Time, he stands firm, unmoved like a slippery rock! (And I hold on, like a slippery rock, among these beating waves. – 'Elopement'). In 1975, I had pointed out in an article, (published in the Mathrubhoomi Weekly on the occasion of the first death anniversary of Edasseri, 'The Dharmavyaadha in Malayalam Poetry'; later, included in my Collection of Essays, 'Sooryakaantham', published by the Kerala Sahithya Akademy) that the 'mukthakam' (slokam - a four line verse) titled 'No Excuse' was the golden key to open the heart of the poetic genius of Edasseri and had observed that Time would wait through centuries to contemplate and realize the essence of the deep, sapient vision of Edasseri. Now, when I look back from 2025, I am tempted to say that within this short span of five decades, the discerning lovers of poetry, though very few in my language, have gradually started to fathom the depths of his writings with awe and wonder. It may be because the Time is rolling off too fast; may be, perhaps, due to the fact that the din and high noises of those Times have subsided, followed the feet that made them, and the stage is now set for candid contemplation. I was trying to explicitly express the significance of this book, which contains a short biography of the Mahakavi, his ten poems and two essays dexterously translated into transparent English. The biography has portrayed a clear picture of Edasseri the great poet, and the compassionate friend of the suffering that he was. He could weep and laugh, and hence could write poems.

'Go; Go and write poems one after another,
For you can weep and laugh.'
(A Presidential Speech - Edasseri).

The biography leads you through the long thorny path of life, 'full of ups and downs and dark holes' that the poet trudged along, to reach the heights. It serves the younger generation of our society as a valuable text book from which it can imbibe the spirit of Karma, imbibe the truth that one endowed with unrelenting and studious hard work, one nurturing great aspiration, can conquer glorious heights, realize great dreams, become successful in life, and can turn out to be a role model for others to look on and strive to emulate. For this, the basic quality one needs to possess is the innate ambition to conquer The Everest.

The two short stories published in the previous collection, titled "The Buddha, I and Leopard", viz: 'Fried Poison' and 'Forty-one Beauties' were written decades ago - the first one in 1926, when Edasseri was aged just twenty and the next one around in 1940. The technique of story-telling in Malayalam literature has undergone sea-changes since then. But these stories declare themselves relevant even today because of the throbbing life depicted in them. Furthermore, they also assert that the basic element that makes a story worthy of note and also transcend Time is not the telling-technique, but is the depth of human life detailed in it.

That Edasseri is a master-artist in portraying human life with all its varied imaginable hues is well established in the realm of his poetry. There are only few poems, like 'Building a House', 'Worship of Beauty', 'Kuttippuram Bridge' etc. which does not have for their content intense inter-actions of incidents in human life. Whatever be the core idea of a poem, Edasseri ruminates over it and gives expression to it developing it into a profound human story. He himself has frankly admitted that many of his poems belong to that particular genre of poetic narratives of story poems. He writes, 'Since many of my poems are narratives, I focus initially on the characters and scenes only, that are required to tell the story.' (My Workshop). Here, I clearly hear the blaring of the warning bell, which cautions me against the misconception that Edasseri's poems are versified short stories. No. It is not so. Actually, they are more akin to drama. (Edasseri has won for himself, to be possessed eternally, his worshipful chair among the dramatists in Malayalam, with his well acclaimed drama, 'Collective Farming' alone; though there are some other dramas also to his credit.) But that is not my point here. Unlike other great Malayalam poets, Edasseri conceives, it appears to me, an idea and develops it into a grand poem with powerful dramatic element being breathed into it for its life-force. Some of his poems (like 'Hanumaan in the giganticide of demon Lavana', 'Wedding Gift' etc. are consummate dramatic monologues, while some others (like 'Blessing', 'The Shepherd of King Bimbisaara' etc. are developed through incidents quite dramatically.

Let me point out incidentally, the dramatic element in Edasseri's poems (not the Dramas of Edasseri) is a challenging research topic that will wait through decades for an enthusiastic scholar with deep insight into Malayalam poetry. The salient point to be noted here is that these two short stories, though written decades ago, attract us even today. We see Time standing with folded hands before them. A close, heart to heart reading of his poems will leave any prudent mind with the impression that Edasseri is an erudite scholar and that he has done in-depth study of our ancient literature, our Ithihaasaas and Puraanaas - especially the Mahaabhaaratham and the Raamaayanam. The warp and woof of his concept of dharma, of the aatmakarma is derived from the Mahaabhaaratham. Quite a good number of his poems can be scanned to establish the influence of the Raamaayanam. Take and squeeze them, you will get the very essence of the Raamaayanam. Even the telling command of language - both Malayalam and Sanskrit - that can be observed in his poems speaks volumes for his scholarship. He could prove himself to be the scholar that he was as mentioned above, earning the whole store of knowledge, all alone with his sweat. He thankfully remembers his childhood days and the atmosphere of his family, pregnant with the culture of the grand epics of India. 'In my childhood, my mother insisted that I read the epics Mahaabhaaratham and Raamaayanam, composed by the great poet Thunchath Raamaanujan Ezhithachan. The erudition or knowledge base that I inherited from Ezhuthachan, together with the tunes that my mind imbibed from my mother's singsong recitation of those epics has sown the seed of my poetry.'

Only one with earnest thirst for knowledge, with intense passion for poetry, with unbounded capacity to dream great dreams, with an unflinching determination and steadfast endeavors to realize the dreams, can grow to the glory of the Viraat Purusha we have seen in the beginning. 'How I could write poems, you may ask', Edasseri continues to write, 'There is no magic in it. It is not due to any extra powers bestowed on me by the deity I worship. My capital for writing poetry was the inherent passion, blessed by the favorable climate.'

In one of his articles titled 'My Workshop', Edasseri discusses, searching through own experience of writing one of his well acclaimed poems, 'New Harvest Clay-Pot and Sickle', how a poem is born; how a poem is evolved from its first spark in the mind of the poet to the final glowing piece of art, with all its aesthetic grandeur. Even the creator himself will not be fully conscious of the final form of the poem he is writing. Edasseri has no doubt at all that, the form and content in a poem take birth in the creator at one and the same time, as an inseparable life force. Aestheticians of the west too will subscribe to this idea. '… in a poem the true content and the true form neither exist nor can be imagined apart. When then you are asked whether the value of a poem lies in a substance got by decomposing the poem, and present, as such, only in reflective analysis, or whether the value lies in a form arrived at and existing in the same way, you will answer, 'It lies neither in one, nor in the other, nor in any addition of them, but in the poem, where they are not.' (Poetry for Poetry's Sake - AC Bradley - Oxford Lectures on Poetry - p.16). To be more exact, they are not two different elements in the making of a poem; in a genuine poem, there exists neither form nor content; there is only poem. Form and content are just two tools in the workshop of criticism to help analyze a poem. Edasseri writes: 'I had searched my workshop several times, prior to writing this essay. Do the form and content in a poem take birth simultaneously? The examples cited earlier do not give me a chance to doubt that it is otherwise. Not only that; no instance is coming to my mind, where I was looking for the form while keeping the content in mind or vice versa.' (My Workshop).

Edasseri has full confidence in his words, the words he used after comprehensive and intense contemplation. Hence, he will say, 'Unless there is a severe grammatical mistake or a slight inappropriateness, I prefer not to change any verse. I will argue that, for the ever-growing language due to constant interaction with other cultures, grammar has got only historical significance. But appropriateness is something that cannot be compromised.' (My Workshop). All aestheticians, ancient and modern alike, will undoubtedly declare that it is inappropriateness that mars the grandeur of a poem. Anandavardhanan has written that 'Anouchithyaadruthe naanyad /

Rasabhangasya kaaranam'.

Out and out Edasseri was an ardent follower of Gandhiji despite the fact that he was not a Gandhian, in the strict sense of the term. He has declared Gandhiji as his Guru and has admitted that it was Gandhiji who molded his inner being. He says: 'Gandhiji is the sole living being known to me, who has seriously studied 'human life' in its entirety. Therefore, if I had any transformation in my life that can be termed as 'development', the inspiration behind it could not be from any other teacher.' All the Gandhian principles that he found worth following were strictly adhered to by him, in his writings and in his private life too. Nevertheless, those aspects of the Gandhian ideology which he believed to be unsound or unwholesome were looked askance at or subjected to severe criticism. During those days, political ideology in India was not as divided to bind together into different collectives or co-operatives of splinter pressure groups centered around individuals, clearly motivated by personal agenda, as of today. Consequently, he was stamped as a Communist by the Congressmen; and as a Congressman by the Communists. No harm if both are judged to be correct; or rather, incorrect. But reality is beyond the boundary of both! See his words: 'Even though I have not portrayed Gandhiji as an individual, I have not written even a single line in literature without keeping him in my mind!' Elaborating the point, he continues to write: 'My writings reflected my complete views either as approvals of or as disapprovals of the Mahatma's ideologies and vision. Those works that reflected my approvals on Gandhian ideologies made a critique label me to the extent, 'an incorrigible optimist'. There were a few others who proclaimed I was 'Communist', in view of what I have written disapprovingly. The basis for both the views is my likes and dislikes about Gandhian philosophy that I am still studying.' So modest is he as to claim that he is still a student of Gandhism. Nonetheless, he will say 'NO' to Gandhiji too, if any word or action of the latter takes away the sacrificial lamb from the altar in the name of compassion, without offering the butcher a different means for life. Only when you do that you merit the moral right to prevent the aatmakarma of a butcher. This philosophy has its deep roots in the epic Mahaabhaaratham; and Edasseri has imbibed the very spirit of the Epic to the full, as has been observed earlier. The core of the mukthakam referred to 'No Excuse', is this philosophy. A comprehensive study, keeping the mind vigilant on the political under-current thereof, of the great poem 'Budha, I and Leopard', particularly in the political scenario of those times, will clearly help elaborate the point. The fore-note the poet has written to this poem will offer you the key to open the heart of the poem, or rather of the poet himself. (Here, one point: Edasseri has written fore-notes to many of his poems, without which no reader can hold breath enough to dive deep into the core of those works. All the fore-notes taken together, along with the poems concerned will afford sumptuous stuff to ruminate to a discerning critical acumen). Even the noble Gandhian idea of Ahimsa is put to test here and proved to be meaningless and obsolete before the primary duty - the aatmakarma - of a father. And, there stands Edasseri, the Viraat Purusha!

Let me break open my heart and show the truth. I feel the warmth of the palms of Mahakavi over my head in blessing. To the earnest readers, I need only say: You have reached the holy gate; bow and enter, please!

Note: K.V. Ramakrishnan retired as Professor and Head of the Department of English, is an eminent poet, essayist and translator. He is a well-known Shakespearean. He has to his credit 42 books, including 4 works in English. He is honored with 13 literary awards including the coveted Kerala Sahitya Academy award for poetry twice. For more information, please visit https://www.kvramakrishnan.org

Preface

EDASSERI GOVINDAN NAIR

EDASSERI - A SHORT BIOGRAPHY

In his life time Edasseri did not write his autobiography; probably he left that task to others. In our endeavour to make this biography as close to his life as possible, we have taken references from his own published essays and interviews, reminiscences by his friends which are published, recollections of Edasseri's family members and also a biographical study by P. Krishna variyar titled '*Edasseri - Poetry and Life*'. A few of his works have also been briefly mentioned herein, contextually.

Edasseri Govindan Nair was born on December 23rd 1906 in Kuttippuram village of the Malappuram disrict in Kerala. His house was situated near the river 'Bharatha Puzha', also known as Perar or Nila. Edasseri spent his early days in the proximity of this river; so, this river had a special place in his heart. When a bridge came up across it in 1953, Edasseri wrote the poem 'Kuttippuram Bridge'. This poem may be the first of its kind in Malayalam raising concerns about the adverse impact of urbanisation on human lives, values and also the environment. Edasseri had one leg slightly deformed at birth. He had to be carried to school and back. Gradually, after undergoing a painful regimen of massages he was able to walk properly. This experience inspired him to write the poem titled ' included in the book, "The Buddha, I and Leopard", which extols the art of celebrating life with all its shortcomings.

Excerpts from Edasseri's essay 'My Poetry' provides authentic information about his early life. 'I used to read daily the great Indian epics Ramayana and Mahabharata from a very young age. While studying in lower classes I had learned by-heart, the *Slokas (verses usually comprising four lines)* from 'Shreekrishna Charitam Manipravalam'. These readings might have helped me in internalizing the craft of poetry. But what really made me contemplate on penning a few slokas were the then popular 'Ammayi Slokas', a mocking term for poems shallow in nature and meant mainly to titillate the reader. In fact, I had written a few slokas imitating them. I do not recollect most of those slokas now; but there is one, a very old one, that still lingers in my memory. Being the monument of my romantic childhood love, I should not forget it! The lover in this poem was ten or eleven years old then!

> *Girl with honeyed words,*
>
> *I passionately wait to see you;*
>
> *The somewhat displaced clothes*
>
> *Worn in haste,*
>
> *Tender body indolent,*
>
> *Perspiration at the base of breasts,*
>
> *Gait of an elephant in musth,*
>
> *And the face that gives much joy!'*
>
> *(Randu Mukthakangal (2) – Edasseri)*

With the collapse of feudalism in the early part of the twentieth century, many of the powerful Nair families (Tharavadu) had decayed and were falling into the clutches of poverty. Edasseri Tharavadu was no exception. Edasseri's short story 'Poricha Nanju' (Fried Poison) throws some light into the pathetic situation prevailed in Nair families of that time and how poverty affected even family relations. To make the situation worse for the family, his father Krishna Kurup lost his life in 1921 to a brief illness in the form of fever which lasted just two days. As a result, Kunhikutty Amma, his mother was not able to provide higher education to her child. Edasseri has in his reminiscence noted this sad situation thus; 'My mother fervently wished to send me to high school. As for me, I wished to feed her at least plain gruel. Both these sentences are complete in themselves.' Edasseri then went to Allappuzha along with his maternal uncle.

He wrote: 'It was during my stay in Allappuzha that I started learning consciously, the early lessons in poetry while I was also learning how to eke out my livelihood. The job provided nothing beyond an assurance of daily meals. It was at that time that poetry with its mighty magnetic power pulled me into its circle. It was during 1925, that I chanced upon a young man by name Manjoor Parameswaran Pillai, who became my bosom friend. He was a person who was passionate about poetry and a connoisseur of literature with great erudition. My prime investment in literature, which I continue practicing, is the wealth that I received through the constant literary interactions with my friend. Manjoor trained me like a mother teaching child how to take his first steps. Whenever opportunity arose, we walked on the beaches of Alappuzha or roamed around in lonely places of the city. Invariably, our topics for discussion used to be poems and poets. And, making poems was our hobby. We used to create on-the-spot slokas and recite them. While I recite the first two lines of a sloka, Manjoor would complete the balance two lines. This way we even made a full poem with fifteen stanzas. As mentioned earlier, during our self-training sessions, we made slokas together. This further evolved into both writing poems together based on a composite theme for each poem. Parted our ways around 1928-1929.

My taste was gradually getting relocated from Venmany's Ammayee Slokas (erotic poems) to the philosophical verses of Sree Ramakrishna, and from the Sanskrit verses of Pandalam Kerala Varma to the verses in vernacular of Kundoor Narayana Menon. The first one did not influence my style of writing. But the second one did leave an indelible mark on my style of poetry. Result was:

> 'To whichever stages you send me
> After teaching me the histrionics
> Needed to enact this amazing drama,
> No questions would ever be asked.

Nevertheless, don't dole me out in front of
Full bosomed ladies, to make me do
Monkey tricks in front of them,
O'! Chieftain's kind hearted daughter!'
(Randu Mukthakangal (1) – Edasseri)

The chieftain's daughter had the smartness to reject this prayer outright; the seeker's smartness was to father six kids and the readiness to perform any amount of monkey tricks!

Those days, I was under the impression that for someone to be a poet, he should at least hold a degree in language (Sanskrit). That was the belief, not only for me but for most of my contemporaries. However, Shailajananda Swamy of Sreeramakrishna Mission, once happened to see one of my poems 'Radha of Vrindavanam'. He sent that poem to Subramonian Thirumulpad who at that time was running a publishing company in North Malabar; Something like a newspaper or magazine. He sent back the poem with suggestions to make a couple of changes. If I remember correct, I sent it back with the changes incorporated. Either my fate was not good or the fate of the poem was not good, that publication was stopped. But that was a realization for me, that my poems are worth considering for publication. And it was a real gain. I continued writing poems; still did not send them to any publisher. Fact is that, I didn't get a mediator like Shailajananda Swamy who would recommend my poems to a publisher. It must have been before 1935; I am not able to recollect the exact year now. A new magazine 'Yuva Deepam' (Divine Lamp of Youth) started publication from a place called Vanneri, near Ponnani. It was in that magazine that my first poem 'Solace' was printed. My friends appreciated that very much, and I was in bliss. (Copy of the magazine 'Yuva Deepam' was later found at the 'Appan Thamburan Library' at Ayyanthol, Thrissur and scanned copies of the relevant pages are now included in the Bibliography on Edasseri's literature).

A person who distressed me equally was Kuttikrishna Marar. That happened sometime later. I met Marar for the first time at a programme conducted by Kerala Sahitya Parishad at Kottakkal. Marar and the great poet G. Sankara Kurup were my idols at that time. I watched them both from a distance. Despite this close proximity, we did not get to know each other. That, in fact was a sort of relief for me at that time. And it was much later, that N. P. Damodaran (who was working with Mathrubhoomi Publications at that time) introduced me to Marar. By that time, many of my poems were published in Atmavidya Kahalam and Mathrubhumi. Despite this, Marar bluntly said that he has not read any of my poems. He had not even heard my name. There was no such occasion in my life where my pride, cultivated secretly and sincerely but covered with politeness, got such a bashing. Strangely enough, I did not feel like leaving him either. And that teacher who returned from Kalamandalam, taught the crazy poet in me who till then was writing without discretion, the art of poetry writing with the much-required discipline. One more thing happened. Strict lessons that I received from Marar was making me rather unabashedly, an imitator of Vallathol. It was Marar himself who gave me strict warning against it. One day, even forgetting myself, I was reciting aloud a poem written by Vallathol titled 'My little Daughter'. Marar recited the following four lines from that poem repeatedly; laughing aloud to the level of ridiculing me. Taking cue from it, my young friends joined in that laughter. It was then that I realized as to how ridiculous my esteem towards Vallathol was turning into. It was like a crow imitating a swan. I consciously started shirking away from those clutches.

> *'Why extend your puny hands*
> *With the longing for flowers?*
> *Someone like you, petite poet,*
> *Won't get even a petal out of it.'*

(My little Daughter - Vallathol)

Up to 1940, I was only worried about how to write poems. Topics were aplenty. I selected instances from great epics as the themes for my poetry. I made poems about nature's wonders. At times, I even created situations and made poems based on that. But I could not turn my face away from the social developments, issuesand the debates in Malayalam literature. Consequently, the way I wrote, took certain detours. I call those detours as evolution of a poet. At the same time, I couldn't stop laughing when I was called an 'atheist' for writing the poem 'Divine Hook' and a 'communist', when I wrote the poem 'Tool down Strike'.

I am yet to arrive at a final conclusion on the theme and the form. On these aspects, I am with my younger generation. And I recollect with pride that I have always been with them. It is with the younger generation that I discuss such subjects. Whatever be the ultimate value of their opinions, those opinions have vigor and life. If these two qualities are lacking, no art form would sustain, so do I believe. Many a time I had felt that my poetry has stunted. At that time, I felt as if my life was a burden - uninteresting and worthless. On each such occasion, I got rejuvenated by reading poems written by my fellow poets. My mind drew energy from them and I felt like my imagination took wings. Advices from the great Bhagavath Gita made me to always engage in karma.'

In Allapuzha, over two months' time, he managed to save two rupees by putting-in extra work as a tutor. With a request to buy a blanket for his mother, this money was entrusted with a trader returning to Kuttippuram. But as fate would have it, one day before this man could reach Kuttippuram, Edasseri's mother who was afflicted with small-pox breathed her last. Edasseri was inconsolable and carried in his heart the burden of the unredeemed debt to his mother throughout his life.

It was my mother who tied

To the corner of my dhoti

All the coins she received

when I was given to the king.

Later when I returned, with

A blanket that I bought, to

Protect her from cold; lo!

She lay inhumed under cover

Of a thick earthen layer…

My life, ever indebted!'

(The Shephered of Bimbisara - Edasseri)

On his arrival in Ponani during the 1930s, Edasseri did not have a suitable place to stay. Those days, lodges and rooms on rental basis were alien to even cities, forget Ponnani. His poet-friend E. Narayanan took Edasseri to his own house, where Narayan's mother wholeheartedly welcomed him and treated him as her own son. Narayanan's untimely death caused deep grief for Edasseri and other friends. At this stage, a well to do acquaintance, Edakkandy Raghavan Nair invited him to stay in his mother's house 'Puthillam'. He was on the lookout for a tutor in Sanskrit for his niece Janaki who had passed matriculation and had started learning the language at home. For Edasseri, this proved to be an important turning point in life. Edasseri married Janaki on the 15th of January 1938. After marriage, the veranda of 'Puthillam' transformed itself into a concourse for holding literary discussions. The introductory note to his poem, 'Worship of Beauty' has reference to the discussions which took place in that veranda.

As mentioned earlier, the strong influence of Gandhi and the uncompromising adherence to principles did not financially help Edasseri. His life was an impossible concoction of poverty, admiration for ethics and adherence to truth. He continued helping his fellow beings in need, many a time even keeping the needs of his family in abeyance. Nevertheless, his own hardships and pains which he identified with those of society were adding strength and depth to his poetry. As recorded by many scholars in later years, his poetry was inseparable from his life. Edasseri valued Nalappat Narayana Menon's literary contributions especially his translation into Malayalam of Victor Hugo's famous novel *Les Miserables*. Acquaintance with intellectuals like Nalappat, E. P. Sumithran and Kuttikrishna Marar exposed him to English literature and more Sanskrit literature. With their assistance and own effort, Edasseri achieved remarkable dexterity with English and Sanskrit languages. P. Krishna Warriyar wrote 'No one can become erudite by mere acquaintance with knowledgeable personalities. It requires effort and commitment from one's own self. Edasseri had both these qualities. He was intelligent and had an exemplary sharp memory. Anything that he heard, read or experienced could be reproduced by him at any given time and without much effort, and he could use them effectively.'

Edasseri took part in the freedom struggle in a praiseworthy manner. Edasseri was the distributor of the underground magazine '*Swathanthra Bharatham*' (Free India) which was proscribed by the British police. Following the Quit India resolution and arrest of leaders, efforts were on to intensify the struggle in Malabar region. It was in 'Puthillam' in 1942 that a secret meeting was held to organize a committee to operate in Ponnani area. C. Choyunni, a freedom fighter from Ponnani, who was jailed in Kizhariyur Bomb case has acknowledged that the freedom fighters like him received considerable courage and enthusiasm from Edasseri. It was the period of Guruvayoor Sathyagraha and Edasseri was totally immersed in the supporting activities in Ponnani. In year 1935, Edasseri along with A. C. Narayanan Vydiar established a library and reading room in memory of their friend and freedom fighter P. Krishna Panicker who died suffering severe torture at the hands of the British Police. The veranda of Krishna Panicker library became the venue for daily meetings for the progressive men in Ponnani. It is worth mentioning that this library is still active and working in the first floor of 'Edasseri Sahithya Mandiram', situated opposite to A. V. Higher Secondary School in Ponnani.

Among the group of freedom fighters were a few individuals who were dedicated to literary and cultural pursuits. Their interactions were also taking place simultaneously. By the year 1936 a group of enthusiasts in literature had been formed in Ponnani with Edasseri as its rallying point. V. T. Bhattathiripad, Kuttikrishna Marar, E. Narayanan, A. C. Narayanan Vydyar, E. P. Sumithran, P. C. Kuttikrishnan (Uroob), Akkitham Achuthan Namboothiri, Kadavanad Kuttikrishnan, N. P. Damodaran, M. Govindan, N. Damodaran, T. Gopala Kurup, M. G. S. Narayanan, P. Anandavalli Amma, T. V. Soolapani warrier, E. Kumaran, T. K. Thressya (freedom fighter and a highly respected teacher who received President's Award) etc. were members who joined at different times in this literary ensemble. The members of this group were avid readers, free thinkers with progressive outlook and above all passionate about literature. They called this group 'Edasserikkalari' (Literary Arena headed by Edasseri), more out of their strong regard and fraternal feelings towards Edasseri. Nevertheless, Edasseri by nature was averse to appear as a guide or leader. They used to debate at length on the finer points in literature and thus evolved a characteristic and defining outlook on life and literature. Edasserikkalari was later popularly known as 'Ponnanikkalari'. Edasseri has acknowledged that his poem 'Worship of Beauty' which celebrates humanism to a great extent, reverberates the serious discussions within the group. In 1940 when Edasseri wrote the poem, he was only 34 years old. 'Worship of Beauty' could be considered as the first sprout of the thought process of Edasserikkalari/Ponnanikkalari; a different way of approaching literature. Later more and more youngsters got attracted to this philosophy.

From his essay Poetry In my Life: 'As far as my poetic development was concerned, that period of four to five years in Alapuzha was the golden period in my life. During this period, I could read many significant court-epics (Mahakavya), long poems (Khandakavya), poems translated from other languages and also could study some of them in detail. I could get acquainted with the initial chapters of many popular Sanskrit poems. By this time, I had already written three long poems (Khandakaavya) named 'Ahalya', 'Malini' and 'Oru Latha. After a lapse of three or four years, Lo! 'Ahalya' was published in book form, but not in my name. The title of the poem and the poet's name were changed! But, I did not object to it. As summer stands-by, ever ready to shower compliments, and the flowers incessantly blossom and drop, what sense of loss a Pooverinji (a tree that produces a profusion of fragrant flowers) would have, if a plant in the nearby bush, not fortunate to blossom, collects a handful of flowers from it to exude fragrance? I was ready to write ten more books of that kind, if anyone wanted! In fact, the 'publishing episode' turned out to be a boon to me. Not only that a poem written by me who does not know Sanskrit language was published, but a renowned newspaper gave a good review of it! Never was there any incident like this, that boosted my confidence to such a level. Followed by this, the poem that I wrote namely 'Janaki' and the Khandakavya 'Malini' written along with 'Ahalya' were published in the magazine 'Atmavidyakahalam' printed under the supervision of the great literary scholar Sreemad Vagbhadananda Guru. Its editor wrote a personal congratulatory letter to me. With this, it was a 'dream come true' for me in the first few decades of the century itself; a dream I thought would be realised only in one of my future births.

My struggle to keep hunger at bay was still at its peak. Only difference was that the scenario now got shifted to Ponnani, a coastal town of central Kerala. My ability to write poems had inflated my pride. But the politeness in my character that I had developed over years of practice could cover up that pride in me like a strong metal shield. Still the consciousness that 'I am unlike others' was growing within me. Even though this feeling gave me the much-needed solitude for reveries, it also isolated me from social circle and opened doors for many misfortunes. I could not do many things, which others could easily do. Even as the cruel canine teeth of hunger was gnawing me, I had to let loose with a sigh, even those easily convertible opportunities. Also, the powerful influence of Gandhism made its mark mercilessly on my thought process. Even while I was loitering without a second pair of dress to wear, without a place to sleep, without a job, or for that matter many things, two individuals needed me. One was E. Narayanan, a budding poet who dropped off before blossoming and the second was P. C. Kuttikrishnan, (Uroob) a student lonely due to inflated self-esteem like me and searching his identity in the labyrinth of thoughts beyond his age. These two youngsters kept me alive; both in life and in poetry.

Life in Ponnani was a replica of Alapuzha; pursuit of poetry forgetting everything else! We studied together and did critical analysis of the contributions of poets who were already established by 1930 and those who entered poetic field between 1930 and 1940. Many a time we delved deep into the realms of poetry and wandered there day-in day-out due to sheer fascination. We did not have any definite aim. Everything was amusing and interesting. I did not learn anything consciously. Nor was I industrious. Now that matters had developed to this stage, I wanted to learn some grammar at the minimum. But, instead of finding a teacher to receive knowledge from, I discovered a disciple to receive it from me. But it suited me. And I started to learn those portions carefully at least for the purpose of teaching her. I could learn from the great critic and essayist Kuttikrishna Marar that poetry is nothing external to life, but a part of the pulsating life itself. It was he who sternly insisted that I speak in my own tone, with my own gestures.

I am a believer of God. But, on occasions when I have to touch upon hunger and lack of love - facts of life which had always nagged me - I find the godly humility and respect towards philosophical doctrines leave me in a jiffy. In the poems by the author who swears by Gandhiji, there lie scattered ideas that challenge Gandhism and even faith in God. The poems which reflected the objective social reality written by me who is a follower of Gandhiji and who has not studied Marxian doctrine, were adopted by the communists as part of their propaganda slogans. One more reason for failure in life: I am a communist in the eyes of the Congress and a Congress man in the Communists' reckoning! But let me not forget that, this benign neglect has helped my quiet poetic life. Poetry also gave me a family of my own. I believe that Bramha (Creator) must have created this girl exclusively for me, the one who was so fascinated with poetry as to copy 'The hymns of Sankaracharya' (reverential poetry) and the translations I had scribbled for 'Pushpabana vilasm' (sensual poetry) in the same note book sans any discretion, for the simple reason that both of them were in verses!

Making money for a living turned out to be the most important issue in my life. I decided to publish my book of poems for which I compiled several of my long poems and named it 'Alakaavali'. Printing was undertaken by Mathrubhoomi Printing and Publishing Company, Kozhikkode that used to publish and continue to publish in their periodicals most of my poems. By that time Mathrubhoomi had started giving me small amounts as remuneration for the poems published in their weekly. That money along with the amount I got from writing legal documents was not enough to pay the printing charges; hence those books didn't come out of the store room of the press for quite some time. Out of the twenty-five free copies that the manager of the press Krishnan Nair compassionately released to me, I sent most of them to prominent poets in Kerala as also to a couple of my friends, and established myself as a poet. I thus achieved the eligibility to dream of a lucky future. Through mediation by another friend, K. R Brothers, Kozhikkode published my drama 'Noolamala' (Entanglement) and gave me two hundred and fifty rupees. The handful of money that I received for the first time on account of literature created wonders in my life! Followed by this, National Book Stall, Kottayam published many of my books. Instead of being a liability, composing poems started to be an income generator. But it never reached an encouraging level.

What do we understand when we say a poet lives? It means that he goes on creating own worlds. Any act at variance with this creative process is considered nefarious by him; however great it may be, as per the 'Dharma Sasthra'. The poet will only be interested to run away from that nefarious act at the earliest opportunity. It is known to everyone that Adikavi 'Valmiki' got an opportunity to do so with the blessings of sages. Here I am continuing with the nefarious act, since my wife refuses to proclaim that, 'The consequence of whatever a person does has to be borne by him alone'. So, my poetry cannot but fail miserably. She is bidding farewell with tears in her eyes while continuously looking back. She is my bosom friend! Rather, she is my known self. I cannot afford to lose her. I have convinced her several times that I am not interested in physical wealth.

> *'Life, noisy each moment like a shack,*
> *With absurdities and sins galore.*
> *They are the offspring of penury!*
> *Lakshmi Devi, the revered deity of wealth!*
> *Falling at your feet, I entreat;*
> *Please do not board, to deliver*
> *Multitudes of your pet miseries too.'*
> *(Moonnu Otta Slokangal – Edasseri)*

These lines written by me were sincere. But she is not content. I have not encountered a conflict of this magnitude at any time in my life. I feel that a solution to this dilemma would be found only when everything relating to me breaks down and dissolve in the earth.'

Edasseri arrived at Ponnani in 1930 and since then, Ponnani became part and parcel of his life; his '*Karmabhumi*'. He was 24 then. Sitting in Ponnani and looking through the lives of the common people of his village, he observed the whole world. He was keen in the political happenings around him and in and around his country. P. Krishna Warriyar has succinctly described the historic context in which Edasseri practised his ideals: 'Edasseri was born and lived through, during a period of change. (Transformation time from slavery to independence for his motherland). The present generation can read in his writings the hopes, anxieties, wants and deficiencies of that period, in family and also in social life. It is doubtful whether any other poet could experience and record those pains as poignantly as Edasseri. Crumbling *Nalukettus (feudal homes)*, all-pervading poverty, the fervour and brightness of freedom struggle, sights of orphaned lives around, social issues with sharp interfaces, the nascent brightness of development - its joy and anxieties - dreams about the future of the nation, the validity of various ideologies, the art and science of life - Edasseri's poems unravel a broad range of issues. In short, it is the social history of Kerala; a window that opens even to India's social history.'

Edasseri observed that during the post-independence period Indian polity had deviated from ideals. This pained him. He related this as the main cause for the sense of despair and lack of direction prevalent among the restless youth of the seventies. He advised them to have grand and worthy dreams, strive to achieve them and not to fall prey to loss of faith and inaction. He wrote the poem 'A handful of gooseberries' in which he says that the youngsters of post-independence era may not be aware of what was gained; but he insists that the younger generation ought to know what they are losing. Edasseri took keen interest in science and astronomy and always tried to understand the new theories propounded by scientists. As far back as in 1959, Edasseri had spread the wings of his imagination to other planets and man's settling there. This great dream preceded cosmonaut Yuri Alekseyevich Gagarin's trip to space conducted in 1961!

Edasseri's family life may be described as blessed. Janaki Amma, with her devotion for literature had deep understanding of her husband's poetry. She was, therefore, the privileged first reader and critic of all poems written by him. She was always the first one to recite for him his poems in her adorable voice. Edasseri has recalled how helpful it was for him when his wife neatly copied in a paper the lines he had scribbled haphazardly. Janaki Amma used to write poems and short stories before marriage. They were published in Mathrubhumi weekly. She had also done a few translations to Malayalam, like Tagore's 'Fruit Gathering' and stories by K. A. Abbas. After marriage she discontinued her own literary pursuits for the sake of her family - to bring up the children and to bring about an atmosphere conducive for the literary pursuits of her husband. The couple had eight children, six sons (Late Sathish Narayan, Late Harikumar, Late Unnikrishnan, Madhavan, Divakaran and Asokakumar) and two daughters (Girija and Usha). E. Harikumar is the famous short story writer and novelist in Malayalam.

On the night prior to the day of his demise, Edasseri was in a joyous mood and played chess with his youngest daughter Usha till late in the night. Next morning (Wednesday, 16th October, 1974) it was breakfast time when Usha brought his food to the table. His wife was sitting beside him. Edasseri had barely started taking the breakfast when he collapsed on his wife's bosom due to cardiac failure.

Collection of poems:

Alakavali (Ornations) -1940

Puthankalavum Arivalum (New Harvest Pot and Sickle) - 1951

Laghu Ganangal (Light Songs) - 1954

Karutha Chettichikal (Dark Hawkerwomen) - 1955

Thrivikramannu Munnil (In front of Thrivikrama) - 1971

Thathwashastrangal Urangumbol (As Philosophies Sleep) -1961

Kavile Pattu (Song of the Grove) - 1966

Oru Pidi Nellikka (A handful of Gooseberries) - 1968

Kunkuma Prabhatham (The Vermilion Dawn) - 1975

Anthithiri (Sacred Lamp at Dusk) - 1977

List of Plays by Edasseri:

Noolaamaala (The Entanglement) -1947

Koottukrishi (Collective Farming) – 1950

(*Translated into Hindi and other Indian languages*)

Kaliyum Chiriyum (Fun and Laughter) - One-act plays - 1954

Ennichutta Appam (Limited Means) - One-act plays- 1957

Chaliyathi (The Weaver Woman) - One-act plays - 1960

Njediyil Padaraatha Mulla (Jasmine Vine that refused the prop) – 1964

- (*Translated into English*)

Jarasandhante Puthri (Daughter of Jarasandhan) - Radio Play - 1970s

Khatolkachan - Radio Play - 1970s

Complete Anthology of Edasseri's plays - 2001

Collection of short stories:

Edasseriyude Cherukathakal (Short stories of Edasseri) – 2015

(*Two of the short stories are translated into English*)

Collection of essays:

Edasseriyude Prabandhangal (Essays of Edasseri) – 1988

(*Translated into English*)

Honours / awards received:

Madras government Award - Koottukrishi

Madras government Award - Puthan Kalavum Arivalum

Kerala Sahithya Akademy Award 1969 - Oru Pidi Nellikka

Kendra Sahithya Akademy Award 1970 - Kavile Pattu

Kumaranasan Prize 1979 (Posthumous) – Anthithiri

Institutions where Edasseri worked in official capacity:

Kendra kala Samithy - President

Krishna Panikkar Reading Room - Founder

Sahithya Pravarthaka Sahakarana Sangham - Member of the Board of Directors

Kerala Sahithya Akademy - Member, General Council

Sangeetha Nataka Academy - Member, General council

Samstha Kerala Sahithya parishad - Member

Kerala Sahithya Samithy - President.

Acknowledgements

Asokakumar Edasseri was profoundly inspired and helped by Prof. K. V. Ramakrishnan, retired professor of English language and a renowned poet and essayist, Edasseri's sons Mr. E. Madhavan (Retired General Manager, Reserve Bank of India), Dr. E. Divakaran (Retired surgeon of Kerala health services and Director of Institute of Palliative Care and the President of Solace, a voluntary organisation from Thrissur supporting children with long term illness) and Mrs. Jayasree Asokakumar - a budding poet who writes in English.

Prologue

BEAT OF THUDI AND CLATTER OF CHILAMBU

EDASSERI

I shall try to document here some minutiae which still linger in my memory related to my small poem 'Poothappaattu' (Ode to Pootham. The fifth poem included in this book.)

An invitation was received from All India Radio, Kozhikkode, to recite a poem for broadcasting. There was enough time for composing the poem. May be because of that very reason, the matter had almost slipped off my mind. When I received intimation from All India Radio to send the script, my mind was blank and I was in a state of panic. I did not know what to write. I did not have even a feeble rhythm on the strings of my consciousness!

There is a famous stanza from an old Malayalam poem starting with 'my daughter shall have none less than a noble king'. Similar is my literary aspiration. The desire to write is intense. But when I sit down to write, I don't have sufficient time; don't have enough concentration; don't remember anything I had studied; no books to refer to; no apt words coming to my mind; What more; when I finish writing, instead of the noble king, it would turn out to be just the opposite, a rogue!

I must have either walked aimlessly in the courtyard with a troubled mind or stood looking far into the paddy fields which lay bathed in intense sunlight. No distinct or dynamic image got imprinted in my mind that could stir up my imagination. How can a mind where even a pleasant day-dream does not enter, be creatively oriented? I must have been mauled mercilessly by the routine noises around me; noises that normally we never give our ear to while immersed in work, but if heard are those that bring only hatred and despise due to their grossness - chit chat between servants, disturbing sounds that the neighbors make while quarreling, smart talk by the vegetable vendor. Some of these might have affected me on that day too. I am not recalling these from my lucid memory. But I vividly recollect one thing about the moment of the sprouting of this poem. The sound of a thudi beat which was coming from far away, in the midst of all those annoyances. As I heard that veiled, intermittent, solitary and echoing sound coming from the horizon, like that of a woodpecker thudding on a tall hard-wood tree with its strong bills - a sound that you hear while walking through a coconut grove - my mind was filled with creative anxiety. It withdrew itself from all other disturbing sounds around me and attained a state required for meditating on something yet not very clear. It is the arrival of 'Pootham'. I can recognize it from long familiarity. And my mind started murmuring spontaneously; 'Do you want Unni? Do you want Unni?' its strings had acquired the desired rhythm!

(Note: A male child in Kerala is lovingly called unni)

Childhood is full of imagination and is intent on creativity. So, once a childlike state of mind is attained, you cannot help molding some shapes out of mud! I have particular reasons to mention 'a child's environment' when I recollect this poem (Poothappattu). When this poem was first published in the anthology of selected poems, I had written a short prologue with the reminiscences of childhood. As mentioned in that brief note, for a villager who is born and brought up in the first half of twentieth century, the numerous deities appearing in different costumes and characteristics in their court yards were as familiar as the people staying next door. Before the sense of distinction between man, animal, bird and other things get rooted in a child, he plays and quarrels with all of them with a sense of equality. All along, the child's mind enthrones in his imaginary world, even if it is with a shudder, those deities installed in his mind through the grotesque figures and attires he frequently comes across. Thus, the infant imagination expands deep into an unseen realm of the universe as well.

As the Pootham, who brings wellness and prosperity to the family, arrives at the courtyard along with its troupe and its performance is over, the offerings are kept ready. Unni, full of enthusiasm is in front of his mother who brings the offerings. He is not content even after looking at the Pootham again and again. At the same time, he is scared by the sight of Pootham and steps back. Eyes wide open with enthrallment; the little hero is clinging tight to his mother's attire making her forward movement difficult. It is at this juncture that the elders in the house ask the pootham 'Do you want Unni; do you want Unni'. Ever new and charming scene!

Surely this was there in my mind. I don't know when; It must have occupied my mind with all its grandeur but without any specific pattern. Was it an idea? No. It was not even an image. It may be wiser to describe it as something that could act as a catalyst for a mind rapt for creation. But there was nothing to sprout from that alone. It must have remained there awaiting a favorable environment and a dynamic will power, to pop up. I have a feeling, an ecstasy, that the mind had thrown long back to the rubbish along with other seepage, but awaiting the pollen, the favorable climate and an energetic willpower. It had the capability to accept the pollen and reproduce. However, the impregnation is an accident.

I have got an atmosphere really conducive for writing a poem. I could withdraw fully to myself behind the closed doors of my mind; take out the shells from my little pot, spread it out, arrange demolish and rearrange them in various shapes and repeat the same to my delight. An imaginary world of mine as I wished for has emerged, as if out of the pre-dawn haze and slowly revealed itself. Along with this, another very important thing evolved. I have my elder sister, an accomplished story teller who had told me many stories in her singsong voice, lovingly and convincingly when I was a child. My mind was trying to catch up with her style of storytelling. It is a good omen to get clarity on the contours of the world that is under creation along with continuous flow of apt words to describe. Thus, a potentially eloquent object, though of a vague shape and rhythm, has taken shape.

Now, the mind is traversing through the most anxious and apprehensive phase. It is during this period that I start misbehaving pathetically to the height of being ridiculed. Many a time the much-needed solitude is broken. As the toothed disc of the battle for life continues piercing into the flesh, one cannot remain in meditation-mode for long. The way-side pond may be trying to keep its inner self still for the celestial brilliance to get reflected in it, but it has no right to prevent the washer-man from laundering a bundle of dirty linen in it. However, it would continue in its pursuit, incessantly carrying in its shattering little waves the transient images of the radiant face of the sun. But this time, before the tranquility of mind turned murky, I could dish out the first verse of the poem,

'Have you not heard the clamour of brass anklets,

Mingled with the rhythm of the beats of drum?'

I started writing the remaining verses again only after a night's sleep. I was a bit shaken on the thought that the previous night's imagery might have been shattered to pieces. I was not very optimistic about the capability of human mind to rise from the bleeding fresh wounds straight to a world of imagination and blissful thoughts. But, after reciting the first stanza a couple of times, my mind became poignant and I could continue writing smoothly and in quick rhythm. What remained were only intellectual manipulations. I will cite an example that will illustrate the situation. After Pootham was introduced with the basic descriptions, I was a bit confused as to how to start and proceed with the story. I was apprehensive of using prose in between, to explain certain situations; that will prevent the flow of the poem. But All India Radio officials had advised me informally that while broadcasting long poems, the poet was at liberty to use short passages, to explain situations if necessary. As a person still limping in the path of poetry, I felt that the advice was difficult to be put into practice. But my mind advised that it was a good trick. I was once again confused. Finally, I did it with a sinful mind. The first sentence that I wrote was 'Then why are we giving new cloth and grain to this wretched Pootham?' Then I added narrations in the beginning of the poem and in between for sake of uniformity.

It is almost a futile exercise for the author himself to read the script immediately after writing, to assess its effectiveness. There may not be congruence between the imagery that existed in the poet's mind at the time of writing and the finite form that has been transferred to the paper. Much of that existed in the poet's imagination as raw material at the time of writing the poem, has made an exit. Consequently, it is difficult to know from an instant reading whether the poem has acquired necessary lucidity and luster. For me to look at that piece of poem - which later to be known as mine - as an outsider, it is imperative that the favorable circumstances that existed in my imagination for its creation has to fade away. But it is not because of this that I did not feel like reading the poem even once after completing it. A feeling of utter failure haunted me. If an analogy 'like a mother who gave still birth' can be said about a male, I turned my face away from it, having denied of even the pleasure of sorrow. The brakeless wheels of the life's hardship had already started rolling on, carrying me along.

In the meantime, my wife had collected and arranged the bits of papers on which I had scribbled the poem and copied them down in good sheets. No poem can survive in that indecipherable handwriting! I copied that into sheets of glossy white paper in my own good handwriting after making necessary corrections. I read it. Not once, but many a time. Like the money in the hands of a miser, I went through it several times. Once to know whether the poem can be recited in the allotted time; then to check my own voice quality; in fact, each time to enjoy it's beauty. Is it to put a small 'bindi' on her forehead that the charming young lady remains in front of the mirror for ages!

Even after all these, my confidence level was pathetically low, while I was sitting in front of the officer, himself an accomplished poet, in the recording studio of All India Radio.

Published in 'Mathrubhoomi weekly' dated November 24, 1968.

Translated – April, 2023

Thudi is the festive drum of Kerala that makes loud thudding noise.

Chilambu is the thick festive Anklet that makes loud metallic clatter.

'Pootham', in real world, is a folklore idolatry character enacted by a village performing artist who traditionally visits the village homes after the summer harvesting.

Edasseri's wife had legible hand writing. As was his wont, a playful teasing!

1. WORSHIP OF BEAUTY

Many friends' meetings were held; at times on the banks of river Bharathapuzha, at times in Krishnappanickar Library, Balakrishna library, on the grounds of Ponnani Mission School, on the portico of Puthillam and a few other places.
* K. M. Kuttikrishnamarar, E. P. Sumithran, P. C. Kuttikrishnan and E. Narayanan were present. Some views had evolved from those serious debates within this group. This poem is the outcome of the echo (may call it clamour as well) it created in my mind.
Thou create the world imperfect as envisaged.
Infuses grotesqueness in it by relentless torment
Upon the vicious deed born of the sculptor's hand.
If so, a God like that - Allay such a thought.
I, on my part, am in search of the kindness
That applies honey on wounds, the Beauty of
Compassion that thrives in this world.
Leave those regal poets, chasing ethereal beauties,
Such as the sky at dusk or a lake with red lotus flowers,
To deceive themselves; I am not up for an argument.
What attracts me most, oh Humanity,
Is your sublime Beauty, whether it be
In ecstatic madness, or in shrieking grief!
Be it in the blissful eyes of the mother
Breastfeeding her baby for the first time -

The elixir of love flowing out from her soul.
Only you triumph, oh! Beauty!
On the delicate cheeks etched with grief
In the depths of despair, as the radiant light
Born on earth for her fades away.
In the spectrum of hues on the joyful cheeks
As the lady in love coos to her soulmate -
Always a charming smile on her alluring lips.
Or, in the thoughts of the bride imploring
Unceasingly, the return of her husband
Moved out due to her own fickleness.
Wonder oh! Beauty, where you do not thrive.
In the adorable baby toddling with little feet
In the nearby garden, wide sparkling eyes glued
on to the flapping butterfly. You equally thrive
Oh! Beauty, in the great sage standing motionless
Amidst incessant tempests of lust and pleasure.
Be it the haughty aiming revenge on his arch-rival,
Be it in the spineless running away seeking shelter,
Or in the faceless planning revenge in incognito!
Why you shower charm on any mortal, oh Beauty!
Man, Beautiful he is as he is the stage personified
To enact dance of incessantly flowing inner emotions.
Whether they be the most revered or even otherwise,
Consider his expressions as extremely charming,
As long as the measuring gauge is imperfect.
Through lives throbbing under such captivating feelings,
At last, the true Beauty of life is manifested; only then,
Will the universe feel dalliance of God as Beautiful,

Only then is full dedication needed at His sacred feet.

Soundaryaaraadhana – Edasseri – 1940

Translated – January, 2025

Translator's Notes:

* K. M. Kuttikrishnamarar (famous critic and Sanskrit scholar), E. P. Sumithran (A Scholar and the Headmaster, Mission School, Ponnani), P. C. Kuttikrishnan (Famous novelist with the pen name Uroob), E. Narayanan (A brilliant poet who died at a very young age). Puthillam was the house of Edasseri's wife Janaki Amma.

In 1940 when Edasseri wrote this poem, he was only 34 years old. 'Soundaryaaraadhana' (Worship of Beauty) could be considered as the first sprout of the thought process of Edasseri kalari; a different way of approaching life and literature. Sri. K. P. Sankaran writes that more and more writers got attracted to this philosophy all around Kerala. This school of thought is now broadly known as Ponnanikkalari.

Not many poems of Edasseri are translated into English, as it is a challenge to translate those poems into any language (other than Sanskrit) with its loaded words and verses. Nevertheless a few of his poems, his essays and a couple of short stories translated into English can be found in the web site https://www.edasseri.org.

2. NO EXCUSE

Each time I lose myself in the sage's voice,

So soothing and compassionate, full of grace,

Who bends to save the precious little lamb

From the blood-thirsty cleaver sword's choice,

Let my soul be raised again and again

With the ruthlessness of the mantra's trace:

"For protection, alas! The only choice

Is Atma-Karma; No excuse … whatsoever."

Published in the Mathrubhoomi Weekly of July 5, 1942 under title 'Sree Buddhangal'. This poem was later renamed as 'Maappilla'.

Translated – April, 2023

Acknowledgement: Following excerpts are taken from the web.

Story of Sree Buddha.

Gautama followed the shepherd who was proceeding to the palace of King Bimbi Sara carrying the little lame lamb out of the flocks of sheep, in his arms.

Fire started burning on the altar. King Bimbi Sara and a group of priests started chanting hymns. The first little lamb was brought there ready to be killed and offered to the gods. In that cruel and tragic moment, when the life of the poor creature hung by a thread, Gautama Buddha stepped forward and cried, 'Stop the cruel deed, O' king. Spare the lamb and take mine instead!' 'Every creature' he said, 'loves to live, even as every human being loves to preserve his or her life'. Then he preached Dharma to the king.

The king was so fascinated with the words of the Buddha that he obliged and issued a royal decree the next day itself, to the effect that no further animal sacrifice shall be made in future and that all people should show mercy to birds and beasts alike.

Story of Dharma Vyadha.

This story as told to Yudhishthira by the great sage Markandeya appears in the Vana Parva of Mahabharat. There lived a *brahman* by name Koushika. He was well-versed in the *Veda*s, of noble character, and a *tapasvi*. Once, when he was reciting the *Veda*s under a tree, a Balaka bird excreted upon him. Koushika was enraged and looked at it so furiously that the bird lost its life and the next moment, fell dead on to the ground. Koushika felt sorry for the creature and repented his doing.

He got up and went to the nearby village as a mendicant for alms. He came before a house where the lady of the house was washing utensils. She said, 'Please wait!' Koushika waited. Meanwhile, her husband came home and the lady, forgetting Koushika, got busy feeding him. After a while she brought alms for him. Koushika was angry. The lady said, "O revered *brahman*, kindly forgive me! My husband returned home, hungry and tired. I got busy taking care of him!" Koushika said, "You are arrogant! How can you insult a *brahman*, who is like fire? A *brahman* can burn the entire world." Lady said, "I am not a Balaka bird. I am doing my *Atma karma*. So, it is not right for you to get angry and curse me. You are well read and should have known the nature of *dharma*. However, I get the feeling that you probably do not know dharma and *Atma karma* in its entirety. I suggest you visit Dharma Vyadha (butcher) in Mithila".

Koushika went to Mithila and met Dharma Vyadha in the butcher's street. Dharma Vyadha was cutting meat, with big knives. After he finished his work, he told Koushika, "I understand that the lady from the village has sent you here. Since you may not like to stay in a place like this for long, shall we go to my house and talk? Once we reach home, you may tell me what I can do for you". Koushika followed Dharma Vyadha.

After reaching Dharma Vyadha's home, the Vyadha went to his parents who had just finished their dinner, and prostrated before them. After an exchange of pleasantries, the butcher told Koushika. "They are my deities! They are Gods to me. I serve them just as I would serve any God. This is my *Atma karma*. The lady who sent you here also was performing *Atma karma* in the form of her service to her husband". Koushika asked him a few questions about soul and about God, and Vyadha gave him a lecture called the Vyadha-Gita, which forms a part of the Mahabharat. It contains one of the highest flights of the Vedanta.

When Vyadha finished his teaching, Koushika was astonished. He said, 'With such knowledge as yours why are you in a Vyadha's body, and doing such filthy, ugly work?' 'My son,' replied Dharma Vyadha, 'I try to do my duty as a householder, and try to do all I can to make my father and mother happy. No duty is ugly, no duty is impure. In my childhood I learnt the trade; I am unattached, and I try to do my duty well. I neither know your Yoga, nor have I become a Sannyasin, nor did I go into a forest; nevertheless, all that you have heard and seen has come to me through the unattached doing of duty which belongs to my position'.

If you would pay heed to my words, go and serve your parents as well. You have left them behind and have headed out to study the *Veda*s. The aged ones are in pain as you have gone away from them. Get home fast and make them happy! There is no *dharma* greater than this!"

Dharma Vyadha sent the *brahmana* away to his parents. *Atma karma* referred to in this poem, is 'acting in accordance with one's skills and talents, one's own nature – svabhava - for which the one is responsible – Karma'.

3. OUR MOTHER

During Guruvayur Satyagraha (1931-32), Kasturba Gandhi once visited Ponnani, my home town in Kerala. Even then, I noticed her frailty due to old age, rendering her unfit for arduous tasks and long journeys. An involuntary sob escaped me when I read the report that Gandhiji had planted a tender neem plant at her funeral ground (1944) in the courtyard of Aga Khan Palace. This poignant moment inspired the creation of this poem.

Beneath your sacred lotus feet, shall I humbly ask,
O' Devi! Was your long life a contented one?
Srimati Kasturba, your feet with life's crimson
Scaled valleys, summits, and mighty mountains.
Alas! It vanished, along with our fortune pure,
Leaving crimson imprints on our virtuous hopes.
On this arduous Maha-Prasthanam,[1]
You denied mortal desires their pleasure; even
Refrained sipping a handful from cool ponds!
In those enchanting days of childhood,
In the splendid wedding pandal raised by parents
Did you wed Mr. M. K. Gandhi, or O' mother,
Did you relinquish worldly pleasures?
From then until final days,
Your revered feet moved to karma's rhythm.
A dutiful housewife, a loving mother;
Two or three children played on your nurturing lap.
By then, millions sought solace in your embrace;

Orphaned voices, throats parched without milk, cried out.
You set aside your own beloved children,
Extended hands to those orphans,
Embracing them as your own.
As the chariot Bharat advanced towards freedom,
It bore an overwhelming burden of responsibilities.
Sans discrimination, your husband piled up challenges
For the nation's benefit, its religious harmony;
Community service, Harijan Seva, Khadi, and more!
This burden should not rest solely on his aged shoulders;
You stooped, relinquishing feminine weakness,
Supporting the weight of that yoke; a compassionate gesture!
Memory transports me to Sabarmati Ashram
Where the resplendent chariot stood at its gateway.
Many who once propelled it, had departed;
Newcomers, albeit a few, had joined.
"To gain speed, the chariot's wheels
Must veer from non-violence," some opined.
Regardless of arrivals or departures,
You - the parents of this nation -
Held the yoke unwaveringly!
Through salt fields, where red blood sprouted,
Through green fields, where red fire ripened,
Sometimes you traversed in conciliation,
Sometimes in agitation, yet relentless
On the careful path of non-violence.
More despicable than this, your domestic life:
The wife of an incredible ascetic Brahmachari!
Compassionate yet adamant, his adherence to Dharma

Showed you the way out for lapses in guest courtesy.[2]

Hunger strike ensued another day, because

You dared to visit a temple where 'Pulaya' was forbidden.[3]

O' Mother, your domestic experiments revealed

Unique adeptness in service par excellence.

Flavours of successful household management

Could dispel bitterness from women yearning autonomy,

Savouring the nectar of Shilavati's stories.[4]

O Mother, your blessed eyes are forever closed,

Your head -pure from selfless service- rests

On the esteemed Guru's holy lap.

We, the forsaken, became motherless again;

Will the welling tears ever dry, in years to come?

Prostrating at your sacred lotus feet, I humbly ask,

O' Devi, was the long human life gratifying?

Parents endure life's hardships,

Happiness nurture in generations to come.

But will the coolness of the well-being,

Ever reach the soul of the mother,

Who rests eternally under its shadow?

Published in Mathrubhumi Weekly March 12, 1944.

Translated – May, 2024.

Translator's Notes:

Kasturba was born on 11 April 1869 to Gokuladas Kapadia and Vrajkunwerba Kapadia. The family belonged to the Modh Bania caste of Gujarati Hindu tradesmen and were based in the coastal town of Porbandar. In May 1883, 14-year-old Kasturba was married to 13-year-old Mohandas in a marriage arranged by parents.

Later on, in 1906, at the age of 37, Mohandas took a vow of chastity, or Brahamacharya. Some reports indicated that Kasturba felt that this opposed her role as a traditional Hindu wife. However, Gandhi quickly defended her marriage when a woman suggested she was unhappy. Kasturba died at the Aga Khan Palace in Pune, at 7:35 PM local time on 22 February 1944, at the age of 74.

[1] 'Mahaprasthanika Parva' is from Mahabharat and reminds us of the long journey of the Pandavas across India and finally their ascent towards Himalayas, as they climb their way to heaven on Mount Sumeru.

[2] Gandhi received many guests at his house and a particular event transformed the couple's relationship. One day, early in 1898, at the young age of 29, Kasturba's loyalty to her husband and his ideals came into conflict with the traditions in which she had been brought up. An Indian Christian guest of Untouchable parentage did not empty his chamber pot in the morning, unaware of the house rules. Under these circumstances, Gandhi wanted Kasturba to join him in the cleaning of the pots that had not been emptied. Kasturba thus carried the pot outside to empty it but she was filled with disgust and shame, unaware that her husband was watching her. Gandhi was unsatisfied, wanting her to fulfil the chore cheerfully. He told her that he would not *"tolerate such nonsense"*, to which Kasturba replied *"keep your house to yourself and let me go."* Filled with anger, Gandhi took her hand and dragged her to the gates with the intention of pushing her out. (Taken from the web).

[3] 'Pulaya' was considered a downtrodden caste. During those days, they were not allowed entry into the temples.

[4] Shilavati was the wife of sage Ugratapas. Lord Shiva and Parvathi subjected Shilavati to a test of character. Ugrathapas contracted

leprosy. He tortured Shilavati for no fault of hers. The chaste and dutiful wife, Shilavati, ran the household by begging, made no complaint, and nursed her husband sincerely. One day, Ugrathapas ordered his wife to take him to the mansion of the courtesan. While carrying her husband in a basket on her head, Ugrathapas's leg struck Sage Mandavya's head. The sage cursed Ugrathapas, saying that he would die at the next sunrise. To save her husband's life, Shilavati started a penance. She pleaded to the Sun not to rise the next morning, and it did not. This is the power that the dutiful and chaste acquires in the story. She is now able to control the natural forces. The sun does not rise; the universe comes to a halt. Anasuya, the consort of Sage Athri, appeared before Shilavati and requested her to withdraw her penance. And she did so. <u>Ugrathapas died only to be brought back to life by the blessings of the Trinity.</u>

4. THE MIGHTY MOUNTAIN OF ISLAM

Note by the Poet: This poem is in remembrance of my childhood
bosom friend. The story is imaginary.
Hundred percent a Hindu with tuft,
I strictly follow the *Aryan* faith.[1]
I perceive divinity in serpent and cow
And in stone in each sacred grove.
Day in and day out I should stand against
Those who brand me a Kaffir,[2]
The *Anaryans* with their ears not pierced,[3]
Those wearing coloured clothes, the bearded lot.
You tainted the white glory of Kerala,
You also added blood-red in its white glory.
Between us, oh! *Mappilas,*[4]
Everything breeds hostility!

2

It was more than thirty years ago,
This rustic village has since changed much.
No longer exists the primary school,
Nor the nearby tall silk-cotton tree.
Bygone are the green shades of afternoons,
Where, Alavi and I, like two wings of ecstasy,
Roamed hands-on shoulders, cosseting fancy talks
Relishing gooseberries that we picked up
And hurling stones at mango tree.

Where you see the grand mansions today
Were then paddy fields, serene and ripe.

3

Class began at ten on the dot
We sat close by listening raptly.
Recited poems, read out text,
Told the story of the innocent goat.
Discreetly copying from each other
New sums were also finished.
Yet it was not time for lunch break
We pinched each other to stay awake.
If your interest is more in playing,
Go out and play, said the bell ringing.

4

On the wayside stood still
The bullock carts with yokes down.
Lying in the cool shades of the trees
White bullocks quietly chewed the cud.
To convey feelings of intimacy
Cart drivers exchanged obscene words.
With other friends prancing
As if under moonlight glow
We too trooped in mirth carefree
Unmindful of the scorching sun.
Bargained much for the gooseberries
With the grandma serving water.
Teasing the grunting old grandma,
With the loud wart on her nose,
Happily, we walked away hollering.

5

Kunhalavi's father Moideenkutty,
The proud owner of the local tea shop
Where, bunches of ripe sweet bananas hung.
Kunhalavi's mother Kunhippathumma
Was also present in the tea shop.
She would be waiting for her little boy
Making for him rice-cake and tea.
My friend would enter the tea shop
I would wait under the silk-cotton tree.
Vibrant reddish flowers bloomed, on the
Skyward leafless branches of the tree.
As the flowers dropped on to the ground,
Small black beetles crawled flying around.
While busy prank stoning the beetles
My eyes would linger on the yellow bananas.

6

Munching the last morsel of the rice-cake
My friend ran towards me,
Hiding one or two bananas in his dhoti.
The bananas stolen from the shop,
On his return, deceiving his father.
Days went by, and one fine noon
Alas! the secret theft was revealed!
'For whom are you stealing these?'
Shouted Moideenkutty, anger flared.
His beard, dyed red with Mylanchi, [5]
Looked redder as his anger escalated.
His large aquiline nose seemed larger,

As if it protruded more.
With each swish of the twig
Kunhalavi trembled intensely
And, the kids who surrounded too.
Moideenkutty yelled at him angrily,
'For whom are you stealing those bananas?'
My name hung in the balance,
My honour teetering on the edge.
Hundred percent a Hindu with tuft,
I strictly follow the *Aryan* faith.
I nearly fainted, breathless, numbed,
The burning inside consumed me.
His boyish lips did not budge
Tightly sealed, it guarded my name.
Hundred percent my dearest friend,
A noble and staunch Muslim lad,
His body trembled, yet his spirit within
Stood firm like a mighty mountain.

7

Hundred percent a Hindu with tuft,
I strictly follow the *Aryan* faith.
Oh Mappila, if you are my Alavi,
Let us walk, shoulder to shoulder,
Call me Kaffir if it pleases you
Live nobly, ears not pierced.
Observe hundred percent
Muslim practices and faith.
Let us go forward and forward
And reap the life's harvest together,

Good or bad, as fate unfolds.

Let it remove Kerala's pallor

And add luminance of colours.

We, whose faith and friendship are equally strong

Should go forward, only shoulder to shoulder.

Islamile Vanmala – Published in Kerala Jayanthi Kerala Samajam Souvenir – June 1950

Translated – August, 2024

Translator's Notes:

This storyis supposed to have taken place around 1920, the early part of the 20th century. During those days, the caste system in Kerala was so rampant and strict that a person born in a Nair family would not eat from outside. If they go out of the house, they can have food only on return, after taking bath. The poet belonged to the sect, Kiriathil Nair, who are considered elite in the Nair caste. Some extracts from the book 'Malabar Manual' by Logan, Williams, will explain things more. Quote:

"Both men and women are extremely neat, and scrupulously particular as to their cleanliness and personal appearance. The men wear their 'kudumi' or tuft of hair on the top of the head.

It may be noticed that the Malayalis distinguish two kinds of pollution, viz, by people whose very approach within certain defined distances causes atmospheric pollution to those of the higher caste, and by people who only pollute by actual contact. Among the first class may be mentioned the following, and the prescribed distances at which they must stand. (For brevity, that part is excluded.) Among the second class are ranked Muhammadans, Christians and foreign Hindus, who defile only by touch. The highest castes are naturally the greatest sticklers for this observance."

"The orthodox fashion is to hold the nose with finger and thumb and dip completely under the surface when nothing more loathsome has to be washed off than the polluting touch of a European's friendly shake of the hand. This bath is necessary before food can be partaken, or a sacred place entered, or several other acts performed". Unquote:

With the collapse of feudal system by the end of nineteenth century, the land holding class consisting mainly of Namboodiri and Nair had fallen on hard days. Edasseri Tharavadu was no exception. With its land lost in adverse possession, financial troubles set in. Edasseri's short story 'Fried Poison' throws some light on the pathetic situation which prevailed in Nair families of that time. To make situation harder for the family, Edasseri's father passed away in 1921 after a brief illness. Edasseri's family was thrown into a state of utter poverty. Even food was scarce.

1. When the word Arya is used as an adjective to denote a quality or character, it means worthy, respectable, honourable, noble and high. Those who did not belong to the group of Aryans were called Anaryans. The word was also used to denote uncivilized or objectionable behaviour.

2. Kaffir: A non-believer of Islam faith. It has been a contentious word. It has benighted Hindu-Muslim relations in India. It has injured the Hindu psyche and made them resent it as a slur.

3. Pierced ears: The ear piecing ceremony was a ritual performed by all Hindus, irrespective of caste and gender.

4. *Mappila*: A person belonging to the Muslim community.

5. Mylanchi, also known as Mehandi is a paste created with henna, that gives red colour to the skin or hair.

5. ODE TO POOTHAM **

(Mathrubhoomi weekly, April 1953)

Prelude:

During childhood days, my close familiarity was with deities than my neighbours. The apparition of the 'patriarch' wrapped in crimson woollen blanket in our prayer room diligently listening to my obstinate crying; the spirit of an ancestor draped in pure white, wandering in the moonlit courtyard fragrant with jasmine flowers; the deity by name 'Bhuvaneswari', whom my elder brother propitiated by offering *'Thanneeramrutu'* (nectar of water) chanting mantras in low tone to the resonating sound of holy bells; another brother as he at times stumbled home late at night inebriated and frightened, lying on the veranda for some time and after gulping down cool water from the bronze jar, narrating his encounter with *the Yakshi* (alluring female fairy) exuding fragrance of jasmine flowers as she sauntered along her course of visitation, and how he narrowly escaped her enchantment; the stories, my elder sister, a master storyteller, spun about the naughty spirit behind the mysterious speck of light during nights known as the 'will-o'-the-wisp'* visible through the open low-level windows of our ancient village house; The numerous 'Poothams' visiting every village courtyard during summer, affirming the existence of such supernatural powers. Frankly, my bond with them surpassed any other in this world.

The concept of 'Pootham' in this poem emerges from the mages of my childhood mind, like the tangled and esoteric phosphorescence of the 'will-o'-the-wisp'. The narration, reminiscent of the style of story-telling of my sister who never wrote a poem.

Sacred lamp is lit. Evening prayers are chanted. Minds half-awake, multiplication tables[1] are also recited. It is not yet time to dine. Don't sleep. Listen to a song about the mischievous spirit; the Pootham.

Have you not heard the clamour of brass anklets,

Mingled with the rhythm of the beats of drum?

Lo and behold the grand arrival of the dark Pootham,

Wearing tiny, bright crescent moons on her body.

Large brass studs droop from her ears;

Fanciful ornaments clang around her neck.

The dark Pootham wears a large headdress,

With tassels festooned in resplendent colours.

A garland of natural flowers slides prettily,

Upon her curvaceous breasts.

Knee-long copper hair let loose,

Veils the shape of her back complete.

Red velvety cloth on her upper body,

White skirt with bells clinking around waist.

Behold the grand arrival of the blessed Pootham,

She dances with stunning allure!

Where is this Pootham coming from? Listen closely:

On the other side of the Parayan hill, [2]

Beneath the rocky ledges on the slope,

Pootham dwells throughout the day,

Staring vacantly through the tiny window,

With her protruding saucer-like eyes.

Young cowherds seek shade,

Beneath the cool grove at noon.

Swiftly emerges the crafty Pootham,

Suckles the udder of a wayward cow.

As dusk unfurls its fragrant veil,

Pootham misleads those hurrying home,

Leads them astray into distant realms,

And she collects betel-quid from them too. [3]

Once the will-o'-the-wisp misleads, the wanderers astray into forgotten paths. If they are to awaken to their folly, they need to place betel-quid on the wayside. As they depart, the spirit would appear, chew the betel-quid, and scatter-spit on the ixora shrub's bushes. That's how the ixora flowers bloom crimson!

In the midnight cosmos' loft,

Where only emptiness prevails,

Magic lanterns are lit in arrays.

She stands languidly by wayside,

Smoothening tangled hair tresses,

A coy smile graces her pretty face.

Wicked youth wander into late night,

Lured and skilfully led by her artful tact,

On the palm's summit, they're positioned,

A seven-storied mansion, it seems to them.

As they slumber ensnared by her magic touch,

She drinks their saline crimson blood slurping.

Bones and hair are scattered on the hard rock,

On the other side of the Parayan hill.

Wonder why we are offering rice and dhoti to this wretched Pootham? Ah, my dears, it would be a sin not to. These were done by the Pootham long ago, and now she harms no one. Pootham is forever melancholic. Why is the Pootham so sad? Listen;

In a mansion, on the bank of the river,

Unni was born after fervent prayers.

His waistband of gold jingled with bells,

Tiny trinkets adorned his ears.

Nangeli fed him food and milk,

She also gave him dolls to play.
Calling crows and cats in her singsong voice,
Showing the bright moon in the sky,
Nangeli fed Unni, rice kneaded in buttermilk.
Would ants sting if left on the ground?
Would lice wander if kept on the head?
Upon the silken sheet, on a cot of gold,
Singing lullabies, patting chubby baby thighs,
Nangeli dozes off, lying on her side.
Unni turned seven, mind swift and nosy,
Yearning within grew for going to school.
Nangeli wrapped the thin-lined border dhoti,
On the white rippled boyish tummy.
Secured his tuft-of-hair with a vine. [4]
Then, she tenderly wiped his bright cheek.
A metal stylus with a golden knob,
And a smoothened palm leaf in his hand,
Nangeli watched Unni from the gatehouse,
As he strolled through the paddy field,
Reached the corner, entered alleyways,
Until he disappeared beneath the pipal tree;
Its canopy spread like a large pandal.
Unni ascended the small hill's crest,
He saw calves and cows grazing.
Ixora flowers beaming amidst green shrubs.
A flock of lambs playing on the barren rocks.
Black beetles encircling the blossoms of,
Red-poon, mountain-ebony and other trees.
Unni strolled forward as the path unfolded,

Unni saw the Parayan's Mandakam. [5]

Then, in confident strides he did slide,

To the other side of the Parayan hill.

At that moment, the Pootham unfurled,

The wee window of the rocky crag.

Pootham beheld the boy strolling,

A night-blooming water-lily

Drifting in a gentle ramble,

A crescent moon wavering in delight,

A golden pot, a ripe Poovan banana. [6]

Within the Pootham's bosom, a tickle stirred,

Goosebumps rising, emotions anew,

Transformed herself into a lovely girl,

She found her place beneath a blossomed tree.

Then the Pootham spoke to Unni in a coquettish tone:

"Unni, my darling, my beloved,

Oncoming sunbeam of golden hue!

Into the thicket, cast away

The stylus, palm leaf, and come to me."

"If I throw them into the thicket

Teacher would surely quarrel with me,

Sweet little girl weaving allure,

Sitting beneath the blossomed tree."

"Unni, my darling, my beloved,

Oncoming sunbeam of golden hue!

In the breeze under shade of the tree,

Sitting on the blue foliated rock,

As smooth as a black beetle's outer shell,

We shall write on tender mango leaves

With tiny silver jasmine buds.

Fling the stylus into the thicket and join me."

"Sweet little girl weaving allure,

Sitting beneath the blossomed tree,

Here I toss into the thicket,

The stylus and the palm leaf."

Unni then did not go to school. He must have thought it to be a joy forever. Now listen. The stylus is made of iron. The moment iron was discarded, the spirit, the Pootham, came and slowly took him away.

Day light waned; rays softened to pale gold.

In the courtyard of the horizon,

The white clouds now blushed crimson.

The child away for study has not yet returned,

Nangeli's silent tears churned with concern.

Along the riverbanks, she wandered,

Calling Unni by his name.

The minnow fish darting and frolicking,

Stood motionless in the river flow.

None in sight, mother meandered,

Her voice echoed through the vast fields.

New sigh arose from beneath the ploughed earth.

Along the hill slope on the jagged rocks,

Mother was disconsolate in search of Unni.

Small owls peered asking, "What? What?"

She trod on to the hill-top and in to the thicket,

Not seeing, the mother kept on walking crying.

As Pootham sat beneath the blossomed tree,

Enjoying stringing flowers into a cute garland,

Along with the adorable Unni,

She heard the saddest of these sobs.
She was least affected. But this nuisance needs to be stopped.
Pootham tried scaring away the mother;
The mother stood serene, and composed.
As a whirlwind, the Pootham swirled,
Mother remained firm, like a stump.
A looming wildfire, scared the Pootham,
With her tears, the mother put out the flames.
Pootham took forms of tiger and leopard
Mother adamant, demanded her child back.
It didn't work. So, Pootham changed her tactics.
As easy as plucking a pandanus flower,
Pootham removed the big flat rock
Revealing the treasure cave in the hill.
Unfolded in it lay dazzling heaps,
Of gold, Jewels and precious stones.
"Gold, jewels and precious stones,
I'll share in a bag-full, but
This child in return, shall be mine."
Not looking at the gold ornaments,
Not looking at the precious stones,
Mother plucked her own eyes.
Like morning red lotus flowers,
She offered them to the Pootham,
Made this plea with folded palms;
"More precious than these is my darling,
Give him back to me, be kind and gracious."
See how clever the Pootham is! Mother has lost her eyesight!
Pootham severed fig from a Thechi shrub,

Then chanted mantras with ardent whispers;
Thus, another child came into being.
In grace, Pootham urged the mother to take.
Mother, in affection, kissed and embraced,
Caressed the boy's head again and again;
Then the mother declared in a jiffy,
"This is not my own!"
Mother reproved Pootham for betraying
The womb that gave birth to the child.
Anger surged within the mother's core,
Hand raised, a damnable curse she'd throw!
Pootham wary, trembled with fear,
Returned the precious child in a haste.
"No longer will I hold your child, O Mother,
Contain your rage, don't drain my Vigor.
Your eyesight will now be restored,
Confirm that this is your child."
Pootham stood trembling, palms folded,
Retreated tamed, wholly defeated.
Before the very own eyes of the mother,
Unni stood, in his true essence,
Radiantly beaming like the moon,
Smile spreading a cool embrace!

Indeed, the mother reclaimed Unni. But what about the Pootham?
Poor thing!

Cradling Unni, ready to depart,
Pootham kissed his head many a time,
Saucer-eyes welled, a rivulet of tears,
A sigh of sorrow escaped her mouth ajar.

The true mother, who birthed Unni,
Her heart softened with compassion,
Fervently spoke to the Pootham, beaming:
"After the Capricorn harvest season,
When 'Calama' [7] grains form golden hills
On the threshing-floor of our houses;
When the fields lie dry, ready to plough,
Call on us every year to return with joy,
For bringing happiness to the lovely Unni,
For bringing wellness to our household,
For us to have everlasting wellbeing."
Pootham agreed and swiftly vanished.
Each year, after the Capricorn harvest,
Pootham visits households, seeking Unni's home.
Needs to find the house where Unni was born.
Forgot to ask; Nangeli's silence held the secret.
Perhaps Nangeli too forgot, may be fear arose,
The Pootham would abduct her darling again;
Who knows for sure, the absolute truth!
Pootham, swollen with longing's embrace,
Wanders through households dancing,
A hopeful chase, Unni still elusive.
Treading, frolicking, she goes running,
To the next house, thinking Unni be there.
"Do you want Unni?" echoes again and again;
Villagers tease her, make her dance.
Drum beats in rhythm with its heartbeats,
Short pipes' sound akin to her sobs.
Have you not heard the clamour of brass anklets,

Mingled with the rhythm of the beats of drum?

Lo and behold the grand arrival of the dark Pootham,

Wearing tiny, bright crescent moons on her body.

Poothappaattu – in Malayalam language was first broadcast by All India Radio, Calicut in 1951. Published in 'Mathrubhoomi weekly', April 19, 1953.

Translated - April, 2024.

Notes by the translator:

* Will-o'-the-wisp': Modern science explains the light aspect of will-o'-the-wisp as natural phenomenon such as bioluminescence or chemiluminescence. These lights result from the oxidation of the gases like phosphine ($PH2$), di-phosphine ($P2H4$) and methane ($CH4$) produced during organic decay. So, while these ghostly lights once bewildered travellers, we now understand their earthly origins. Remember, chasing a will-o'-the-wisp might lead you astray, much like pursuing an elusive dream.

** The name 'Pootham' has its origins in Indian (Sanskrit) scriptures. It carries a beautiful meaning, signifying the 'pure self' or 'Pure soul'. In the context of Vishnusahasranamam, it represents the one with an extremely pure essence, unaffected by the impurities of 'Maya' (Illusion).

While a broad approximate translation might render 'Pootham' as 'Fairy', 'Poltergeist' or 'trickster Devil', none of these capture the essence of the real Pootham.

The dance of Pootham is a ritualistic folk-art form primarily performed in the Valluvanad region of central Kerala during Devi temple festivals. In the real world, 'Pootham' assumes different mythical characters in various regions within Kerala enacted traditionally by village performing artists. The performance involves spirited dancing, accompanied by drum and a short pipe. Edasseri has woven a unique myth, both universal and secular, in this poem about the enigmatic "Pootham".

1. It is a practice for children in India to recite multiplication tables after evening prayers.

2. The headgear worn by Pootham is an immensely big decorated semi-circular crown made of palm leaves and is sometimes referred to as 'Mudi'. Various types of dyes are used to decorate the headgear. The peripherals of the headgear are decorated with frills. Pootham wears a face covering, with mouth kept agape and the tongue sticking out.

2 & 5. Parayan and Parayan's Mandakam. Parayan form a caste in Kerala society. Mandakam is a small brick and clay structure, where various types of rituals are performed by Parayans. The people of this caste were artistically proficient in witchcraft and were believed to possess magical powers.

3. Betel-quid is a combination of betel leaf, quick lime and a few pieces of areca-nut. Once chewed, the saliva turns into dark crimson red.

4. Tuft of hair – In olden days, people used to grow their hair without grooming. Usually, the tuft will be tied using a piece of cloth. In the poem, Nangeli uses a piece of vine to tie Unni's tuft.

6. Poovan is a small banana variety cultivated across Kerala. When ripe, it attains attractive bright yellow colour. Ripe Poovan is without any flaw, as it is resistant to fruit cracking.

7. Kalama is a type of high-quality paddy grain.

6. FACING THRIVIKRAMA

Mahabali:[1]
The empire gained by my father
Beneath the sacred sole of Thy foot.
The sole of Thy foot covered over
The realms that my fame acquired.
Brahman,[2] Thy foot ascends anew;
What remains for me to proffer is
Transcendent, unyielding in any tempest.[3]
Like thunderbolt from a compassionate cloud,
The curse you spelt, Supreme Guru,[4]
Dislodged the crown from my head!
I prostrate at Thy sacred feet with head, bared;
May Thou shower blessings on it.
The crown for it henceforth shall be
As light and fragrant as a Tulsi leaf.
Vindhyavali[5], we behold this marvel,
A spectacle the world has never seen,
Undulating, dreadful yet oddly alluring
Nearly impossible for a repetition:
Sun and moon adorning the face
As lustrous ornaments for the ears
Right hand holding a staff
Yuga-Sandhi[6] are its nodes.
Deer-skin draping the chest

Resembling descending Milky Way.
Earth itself crafted the golden pedestal
For Thy sacred feet!
Sages chant Amnaya[7] scriptures,
Jaya-Jaya echoes; heavenly beings
Shower Kalpaka[8] flowers.
With the rhythm of a drum at fast tempo
The monkey[9] circumambulates the Lord
Who measures earth and sky like lightning.
Those who celebrate 'This Day'[10]
As Freedom-Day; your exhilaration
Amuses me, the son of Virochana![11]
For a thousand year,
Not a grain of sand is wet by tears;
Smiles ceased to sprout, say the Sages.
We wiped out tears with our own hands;
We robbed the bloom from every lip,
Say the sages!
With sorrows extinct forever
The sweet taste of joy departed.[12]
In this numbing state, they say,
Life on earth became insufferable!
Rock bunds built as safety measures
Blocked the flow of life's river;
Stagnation spoiled it despicably!
Don't know in which dark cave
The truth of Dharma lies concealed.
Grief, are Thou the absolute truth,
For the sustenance of life on earth?

Brahman! You promised to manifest

Whenever Dharma waned on earth.

But when virtue extols vice,

Deceit assumes colossal form!

Vindhyavali, my virtuous lady,

Tender vine, bearing blossoms hued,

Lean on me, rest your apprehensions

Upon my unwavering shoulder.

Dark abysses, backstreet corners

Where life contorts and groans,

Pits ablaze with hunger and thirst,

Splintered gateways of death,

All are resurfacing from our memories;

Awakened, ready to enact.

But even impervious souls may soften

In fate's ethereal whirling.

Impossible to forget, O virtuous one,

But we slip into it, let us not stumble now.

Enough my enraged lady, convinced am I;

Dynamism in life is the beauty of Dharma!

Truth and Falsehood - its two steps

That propel Dharma forward!

Brahman! For discernable Dharma

I, unyielding in my spoken oath,

Offer with bowed head

My promise at Thy feet.

Thrivikramannu Munnil – Published in 1971.

Translated – June, 2024

Notes provided below are taken from the Web.

1. Mahabali: Mahabali ruled as a benevolent and generous king. His people were honest, healthy, and happy under his rule. He represents the unconquerable spirit of equality and justice for common folk. On that religious site, Lord Vishnu appeared in disguise as brahmin boy 'Vamana' (the sixth avatar), and asked for three steps of land as alms, for him to sit and pray. Sage Shukracharya, who was officiating as the head-priest at the hundredth horse sacrifice, realized that the young brahmin was Lord Vishnu himself. He tried to stop Mahabali from giving the 3-step land to the brahmin. As Mahabali refused to accede, it is said that, Shukracharya embellished a curse "Let your wealth and prosperity be ruined."

2. Brahman: Brahman represents the ineffable, all-encompassing reality - the ocean from which all waves emerge. Realizing Brahman is the goal of spiritual seekers.

3. A world not swayed in tempests: The metaphorical use of 'swaying in the tempest' suggests chaos, conflict, and upheavals in life. This verse in the poem, encapsulates a harmonious, undisturbed existence - a world not affected adversely by the storms in life.

4. Supreme Guru: Shukracharya.

5. Vindhyavali: The wife of **Mahabali** in Hindu texts. She is identified as the daughter of **Himavan.** Vindhyavali exemplified the qualities of a virtuous and supportive family woman towards Mahabali. Descriptions depict her as both beautiful and compassionate, exhibiting a caring disposition towards all living beings.

6. Yuga-sandhi: Refers to the transitional periods between the four main cosmic ages (yugas) in Hindu cosmology and serves as pivotal moment in the cosmic cycle, as it marks the transition from

one Yuga to another.

7. Amnayas are holy scriptures belonging to the Tantra school of Hinduism which is rooted in the Vedas.

8. Kalpaka flowers: In Hindu cosmology, Kalpaka Vriksha is considered as the 'Tree of Life'. Kalpaka flower symbolizes abundance, fulfilment, and divine blessings.

9. The monkey: As per Purana, **'Jambavan',** the wise and venerable king of the **Vanaras**(monkey-like beings), circumambulated **Vamana**at lightning speedwhen He assumed the form **of the magnificent Thrivikrama.**

10. Mahabali said, "O Lord, since you want me to ask for a boon, I do so. Though I go to Sutala in the under-world, I cannot forget the subjects of my erstwhile kingdom on earth. Therefore, let me be blessed to see the happiness of my subjects at least once a year. Thrivikrama granted his request and said: "The auspicious day on which you gave me charity will be celebrated as a festival day on earth every year in future. On that day the whole earth will be the kingdom of Mahabali. People will worship you as a symbol of their ideals and joy."

11. Son of Virochana: Virochana's life was marked by philosophical debates, virtue, and fateful decisions. His legacy lives on through his son, the illustrious King Mahabali.

12. Following is an extract from the book 'Edasseri Govindan Nair' in the series 'Makers of Indian Literature', written by Dr, M, Leelavathy and published by Sahitya Akademy, New Delhi.

'Facing Thrivikrama' (Thrivikramannu Munpil) was first published under a different crest, 'Facing Vamana' (Vamanannu Munpil). Though 'Vamana' and 'Thrivikrama' are the same, their etymological differences signify different aspects. 'Vamana' is dwarfish whereas 'Thrivikrama' is the cosmic figure that could measure out the whole globe in one pace (Vikrama – Pace). Though the story of the 'divine deceit' is not altered, the way Mahabali looks at it is different in the poem. The great universe is the God, Vishnu, before him any mighty human being is infinitesimally insignificant. A righteous person is naturally confounded when he is condemned and finished, on the basis of unfounded allegations. Such is the situation Mahabali finds himself in, when he was deprived of the throne and thrown away in the nether land. The allegations against him are utterly baseless.

Mahabali wonders: What is right? What is wrong? Probably man would not find out. Possibly, sorrow is the eternal Truth. God's promise was to take incarnation when righteousness would be on the decline. But when righteousness conquered wretchedness, God takes an incarnation to justify deceit! Meditation over such contradictions has taken not only the mythological character but the poet also, to the truth of the polarity of opposites. Light is experienced only because darkness exists. Happiness is experienced only because sorrow exists. The poet sees in the story of Mahabali, a symbolic illustration of the truth of the complementary nature of opposites. Vedic concept of 'Thrivikrama' is actually a pointer to this. The three 'Vikramas' (Paces) of Vishnu are mentioned in one of the hymns Rigveda. Two 'Vikramas' are unknown; the third is known. The known 'pace' refers to daytime as Vishnu is the Sun God. The third of the paces refers to night time. Thus, Thrivikrama is the darkness. This, the poet finds are applicable to every phenomenon which implies an opposite.

7. THE COWARD

'As a psychological analysis of the character Maricha from Ramayana,
it is unlikely that any other Malayalam poet has attempted a similar
poem. Surmise is, in other languages also there may not be any!'
K. P. Sankaran (A collection of complete Poems of Edasseri)
Long and wide blue eyes
Full with fleeting expressions
Pristine swift undulations
Spreading golden rays throughout [1]
In the hermitage garden, my image
On each and every tender leaf.
Strange to see deer everywhere!
I am Maricha, the emissary!
Little by little, the timid animal
Hunker within me.
The vile demon Dasha Kanda [2]
Cower behind me.
He is reaching this hermitage,
As divine as a temple,
For collecting late-day alms [3]
Need to lure away by then
The teamed-up twin divine forces.
I see you son of Sumithra; [4]
A ruthless bow with string intact
A palm tree as firm as iron
Guarding the gate, unflinching.

Who's on the blossomed flower bed
In the veranda of the hermitage?
In the slanting amber sunrays
It's a peak with a rivulet on the left.
Beauteous, with the dirt of indulgence
Cleansed off by desiccation in Yajna.
I see before me a family life, with
Utmost restraint as the only affluence.[5]
Is that a bow with its string slackened
Or a stunning lady with her hair astray?
With love, Rama! Your eyes rove
On either side, at the same time.
What was practised till now
And without restraint, Rama;
My composure turns into revenge,
Hood full blown, seeing your bow.
Is it not this 'Kodanda' [6]
That pierced my mother's heart?
Will there be a son, other than me,
Not avenging; a heretic blasphemer![7]
Let me conceal my thunderous roar
In a murmur, to carry out my plan
Like concealing my fierce figure
Under the golden skin of a gullible deer.
With life sucked in by your arrow, Raghava,
My brother Subahu became immortal. [8]
Taking this penance, I have become
A slayer of my own soul. [9]
Here I come, empowered by king Ravana

To catch you off guard, Rama!
You may defend his mighty Chandrahas [10]
But not my velvety deception.
Let the mighty-armed, clamour loud
On principles of noble dharma
Let them in the name of same dharma
Kill women and remain glorious.
The defeated, the weakling, also need
To quench life's dark thirst for revenge.
He enjoys fulfilling his desire
By digging trap-pits at best.
But, will I the emissary, get fulfilment
Even in this wicked act? Alas!
I am Maricha, a mere commodity,
A bizarre animal, in-between the valiant. [11]
Rama, once you spared my life
And I meditated on your form.
How the tree-bark suited me then
Likewise suits the deer-skin now!
If it was your sharp arrows then,
It is the snarl of the ogre now.
Pity, that a coward has to
First discard his own true face.[12]
Coward, as he embraces gratitude,
Camouflages himself with holy Bhasma
When he decides to embrace revenge
He is darkened by the smoke of deception.
Never should I be a cause of humiliation
To the great soul Sunda!

Grandfather! Your grandson [13]
Is doomed to face his own fate!
I have to inevitably play my role
Though the chances of success are feeble!
Mighty Nature provides by default
The type of role befitting each!
In this battle, Raghava,
You and Maricha are alike.
Your arrow for sure will pierce me
But by then, you too will be wounded! [14]
As targets, we inexorably seek
The iron-sharpness of the opponents.
Knowingly or unknowingly, then
Has Nature ever missed its aim?
Undertook penance to avenge; outcome?
Falling at the feet of the enemy for help.
Closed eyes to see the Almighty
Spotted was the epitome of cruelty.
One can immortalise his name
By inflicting pain in this world.
If even that is to be performed
In the name of someone else;
Is there any misfortune worse
That can befall on a coward!
Sky turned blood-red
As if cut into umpteen pieces
By the wings of vulture Jatayu. [15]
Pollen risen with the breeze at dusk
Turned the forest pathways obscure;

A perfect setting for deceit.
And like a series of obstacles
On the rugged path of one's own fate
My twisted hooves are rolling.
Sita, let the clinks of my hooves
Be the sweetened noise for your ears
Which have acquired virtues
Absorbing the vibrations
Of the bows of Rama.
Let my disguise be blessed
By getting mirrored in your eyes;
The eyes that need to resist
Conflicting forces, every moment.

Poem 'Bheeru' - published in the magazine Yugarashmi, 1969.

Translated – June, 2023

Notes by the translator:

[1] Spreading golden rays throughout - In Ramayana, Maricha the son of demon Sunda, assumed the form of a beautiful golden deer, which had silver spots and glowed with many gems like sapphire, moonstone etc. on its body. As the deer gambols, sun rays get reflected all around.

[2] Dasha Kanda – Ravana (with ten heads) was king of the demons. He owned Chandrahas, the sword gifted to him by Lord Shiva.

[3] For collecting late-day alms – Alms given after noon time is considered inauspicious.

[4] Son of Sumithra – In Ramayana, Dasaratha had three wives. Kausalya, Kaikeyi and Sumithra. Rama, the eldest, is the son of Kausalya and Laxman and Shatrughna are the sons of Sumithra. Bharata was the son of Kaikeyi. Laxman was emotionally attached to Rama and Shatrughna was emotionally attached to Bharata.

[5] Utmost restraint as the only affluence – Rama and Sita lost all worldly assets, before being exiled from own kingdom. Their only wealth then was self-control. However, it is not easy to reach the mental state that enables you to meet life's unpleasant experiences, disappointments, and sad moments with even-tempered calm instead of being tossed about like a ship in a storm.

[6] Kodanda - The very large bow used by Sree Rama to Vanquish the practitioners of Adharma. Usually a bow has 3, 5 or 7 joints. Kodanda had 9 joints!

[7] Heretic Blasphemer – A person who only 'claims' to have the attributes of a deity.

[8] Subahu became immortal – When Maricha and his brother Subahu attempted to rain flesh and blood on the sage's yajna, Subahu was killed by Rama. Subahu became immortal, because he was killed by Rama, the God personified. For no apparent reason, Maricha was spared.

[9] I have become the slayer of my own soul – Suicides were prevalent even during Vedic times. However, the Upanishads categorically condemn suicide. The 'Isavasya Upanishad' states that "he who takes his self, reaches after death, the sunless region covered by impenetrable darkness." Maricha knew pretty well that it is suicidal to affront Lord Rama, whether direct, or in disguise.

[10] Chandrahaas – The sword presented to King Ravana by Lord Shiva.

[11] In-between the valiant – Maricha considers Rama and Ravana as valiant. Maricha realises that in between them, he is merely a commodity, an unusual animal.

[12] First discard his own true face – A coward cannot challenge his enemy in direct combat. Identity being the same, he needs to conceal his appearance and take revenge discreetly.

[13] Grandfather – Maricha was the son of demon Sundon and a Yakshini called Tataka. Tataka was the daughter of the Yaksha king Suketu, who had gained her as a blessing from the God Brahma. This way, Maricha's matriarchal grandfather is God Brahma himself!

[14]Wounded – In the context means insulted, injured, slighted, upset, outraged etc.

[15] By the wings of vulture Jatayu - Jatayu is a demi-god who has the form of a large mighty **vulture or eagle**. He is the brother of Sampati, an old friend of Dasharatha (Rama's father). It was Ravana who killed Jatayu.

8. COLOURFUL ATTIRE

Alas, the gusts of wind in the palm forest stilled
The swing we set during Aathira, now frayed[1]
Kamadeva's armoury on the mango bough, sealed[2]
Moist Kumkum anointed on bosoms too is dried up
No more flute's melody, no more moonlit nights,
Yamuna's shores once festive, now rest silent.
Above the kettle-drum's thunder, Panchajanya resounds.[3]
The amorous themes have faded into distant memory.[4]
Paddy field dotted with cows nibbling harvest remnants
Cuckoo's voice dries up in its comely throat.
Has the earth drunk the greenery, in one gulp?
Countryside, a playground for the scorching sun.
Those hopping sacred-grove to grove, chasing festivals,
Are you watching the dances, grasping their essence?[5]
Oracles raucously jangling the Kaduthila sword,[6]
Frenzied howls of the oracles, the deafening fireworks,
Wild dances of Padayani[7], resounding beats of the drums,
A cacophony of uproarious shouts.
Yet the true spirit eludes the picture,
Sitting in Padmasana, eyes half-closed,
Open hands resting upon the thighs.
Stitch a colourful attire to masquerade,
The violence inseparable from the inner-self.

As the Idol fades through prolonged usage,

Should the Deity, not the Idol, be the scapegoat?[8]

"Do the distant boulders, mark the gateway to hell, sages?"

"Rama! They're vestigial skulls of Janasthana[9] sages,

Devoured by Ravana's demons."

"I will quell this cruelty, o' sages; relying on those

Whose inner strength remains unyielding

Despite being steeped in Arsha Culture!"[10]

As rains cleanse deer-blood from the majestic forest,

Sages return to deep meditation.

Autumn smiles, and the sages share their sorrow

Untangling wet silver beards, they spoke,

"See dark smoke rising up from the south;

Hanuman hollers! Poor mortal souls."[11]

Back to meditation, sitting in Padmasana,

Half-closed eyes, open hands upon the thighs.

Varnnakkuppaayam – Published in Malayala Nadu Annual Issue 1970.

Translated – June, 2024

Translator's Notes:

'Colorful Attire' is considered as one of the proud creations of Edasseri. It is not an emotional poem. It is the poet's empirical knowledge, his convictions or rather his vision, that he puts in the following verses.

Stitch colourful attire as a masquerade,

For the violence undetachable from inner-self.

As the Idol fades with time's embrace,

Shall the Deity be the scapegoat?

We are proud that Bharat is the land of sages, and of non-violence. Fact remains that, violence is something that cannot be severed from the true self of human being. To cover it up, you may stitch colourful attire.

The poet does not intent to justify or praise violence. Maybe he cautions us that, however colourful the external attire be, (Chanting non-violence, Proclamation as the land of sages, deep trance sitting in Padmasana posture etc.), the violence inherent in one's own-self cannot be done away with. Best thing therefore would be to be aware of it and keep constant vigil against it.'

Research shows that humans are genetically predisposed to kill each other. Among mammals, the rate of lethal violence caused by members of the same species is typically 0.3%. <u>However, for homo sapiens, it is seven times higher!</u> Our primate ancestors were also violent creatures, exhibiting a propensity to kill their own kind. This behaviour has persisted in our evolutionary lineage.

1. Athira or Thiruvathira is a Hindu festival-day in the month of Dhanu in Malayalam, corresponding to the month of January as per English calendar. It takes place on the full moon night.

2. As per Hindu mythology, flowers of mango trees are the arrows of Kamadeva, the God of love.

3. Panchajanya is the conch of Hindu preserver deity, Vishnu. The conch was used by Sree Krishna the Avtar of Vishnu, during the <u>Kurukshetra War</u>, and is held in popular tradition to have signaled its beginning and the end.

4. The amorous themes of the past indicate the romantic mood it portrays.

5. Only a very few go deep into the subject and understand their meaning after proper analysis. Common people see the drama without knowing its real meaning.

6. Kaduthila: This is a type of sickle-shaped sword, on which numerous tiny bells are attached. This is considered sacred and is used by the oracles in Bhagavathi temples of Kerala.

7. Padayani, (Malayalam word for military formations) is a traditional folk dance performed in Bhagavati temples. A version of its origin is related to the practice of ancient martial arts training in central Kerala.

8. An idol is a physical object usually made by humans, representing the deity, the divine status, quality or stature of a God or Goddess and is installed in sanctum sanctorum of a temple. Every day, the idol will be washed and be cleansed by pouring ghee, milk, turmeric water, pure water etc. After prolonged usage, it may wear out and conceal the original shape. At that time, it is advisable to change the idol with a new one than causing to mistake the deity later for something else.

9. Janasthana is a part of Dandaka forest, which lies in the basin of Godavari river in India. As per Ramayana, during the time of forest life, Lord Rama lived in this place along with his wife Sita and his brother Lakshman for an extended period. It was here that Rama killed fourteen thousand ogres.

10. "I will quell this cruelty, o' sages; relying on those

Whose inner strength remains unyielding,

Despite being steeped in Arsha Culture!"

There is misconception between non-violence and cowardness. Most of the time, cowardness puts on the attire of non-violence. Non-violence has become the safe haven of cowards. Actually, only a valiant can be successful in non-violence. It is the same with Vadic culture. People hide behind Vedic culture, when they are afraid of confronting. Edasseri has written many poems to caution people against this. He has also written the drama 'The Return' (Thirichhettal), based on this theme.

1. As per Hindu mythology, Hanuman, also known as Maruthi, is the son of wind. With the longest leap ever conceived in the history of world literature, he jumped from India to Sree Lanka, which is lying south of India, over the sea. There he confronted Ravana, set fire to many houses, and killed thousands of ogres, leaving Ravana to the mercy of Rama.

9. SACRED LAMP AT DUSK

The Sun reached untimely
The evening seashore, one day.
Intense sprinting of the day,
The green horses lay coughing up blood. [1]
At the veranda of the first home,
The Sun God saw a grandma.
"Reached at dusk, exhausted;
Can you offer a little space
For me to take rest for a while?"
"No…No; if you stay back
Where will the vain darkness roost.
I shouldn't betray my traditions
By letting in the shining light."
Ignominy, the Deity lowered his face.
He then passed through the grand entrance
Asked the frivolous woman, changing
Wet clothes at the South veranda.
"Reached at dusk, exhausted;
Can you offer a little space
For me to take rest for a while?"
Covering her bosom with arms crossed
She said coyly, "If you stay back, then the
Quiet and serene blue night won't come.
If the blue night doesn't come,

My husband will not arrive.
Why then did I unfurl my costume,
Scented with fragrant pandanus?" [2]
A bit more tired, the Deity mused;
'Is it darkness that people cherish!'
His right fingers ran a few times
On the thrice wound sacred thread, [3]
That lay across his chest.
Too tired, the Deity trudged,
Sidestepping the patio.
At the North of the Naalukettu [4]
He saw an adorable young girl
Like a blooming jasmine plant.
Face and legs washed clean
Bhasma applied on the forehead, [5]
She was all smiles, unhesitant,
Like a profusion of compassion!
"Can you kindly extend your finger-tip
As a support for me to walk?"
The Sun God could never ever
Retrace his own path!
The girl was moved instantly by affliction,
A feeling of alienation remained though.
Maybe, she has read about the father of Karna! [6]
Nevertheless, she took a firm decision
Considering the Dharma of this period
To retain shining light in this world!
Out of a torn-out part of her soul,
She spun a wick; doused it in oil,

Then placed in a brass Diya. [7]
She helped the Sun God to walk
Holding on to the tip of the wick, [8]
Like an elder sister helping
Baby brother to take the first few steps.
She emerged from the Naalukettu
Along with the trudging Deity.
Grandma, as she stood on the veranda,
Prayed with her hands folded.
Praying for union with her husband
The married young woman stood
Blissfully, with bowed down head.
The deity, whom the beetles praise intensely
By blowing conch in the jasmine blooms, [9]
The Deity known to be pleased instantly,
Was then installed by the young girl
On the raised platform of the sacred Tulsi. [10]
Even the vainest of pride,
That puts-off prevailing light
Will bow before you youngsters,
Holding the flame of the lamp at dusk.

'Anthithhiri' - Published in Deshabhimani Onam Special issue in 1970.

Translated – July, 2023.

Anthithhiri, Diyaor Sacred lamp at dusk - Lighting a lamp in the evening is considered an important ritual. The oil or ghee in the lamp symbolizes our Vaasanas or negative tendencies and the wick, the ego. When lit by spiritual knowledge, the vaasanas get slowly exhausted and the ego too finally perishes. Light is analogy for knowledge and wisdom. The poem lauds the little girl for her act of generosity and faith that saved the world from eternal darkness. She represents a new generation willing to challenge traditions and to embrace changes.

1. Green Horses – As per Bramhanda Purana, Matsya Purana, Vayu Purana etc., the Sun is travelling in a single wheeled chariot swiftly drawn by Tawny (greenish yellow) horses, seven in numbers.

2. Fragrant Pandanus – Pandan leaves have nice fragrance and are kept in wooden dress boxes by the women. It also has antibacterial and antifungal properties.

3. Thrice wound sacred thread – Sacred white thread (Janeu) is generally worn by a Brahmin. Three cotton threads will be wound together to make a single sacred thread. It is common for Brahmins to pass their fingers on the thread, when in distress or engaged in deep thought!

4. Naalukettu – is the ancestral, fairly large house of Nair community, consisting of various rooms and kitchen with an open patio in the middle.

5. Bhasma – is an ash obtained through incineration and is applied by devotees mainly on their forehead.

6. Karna's father – Reference is to the story told in the great epic Mahabharat. With the help of the mantra that sage Durvasa provided to Kunti, as a reward for her hospitality, she could invoke any God of her choice to have their child. Kunti was not married at that time, But, out of curiosity, she invoked the Sun God. Once the Deity appeared, Kunti pleaded with him to leave her. The Sun God told her that once invoked, he cannot go back without giving Kunti, the boon. And that was the child Karna. Google 'Karna' for more details.

7. Diya – is a small bronze oil lamp, used to light wicks soaked in oil. These are generally used in rituals and also in houses in the morning and evening before prayers. In the original poem, the word 'Sneham' is used in place of oil with the dual meaning of oil and love! I couldn't find a single word in English language that has both the meanings.

8. To walk, holding on to the tip of the wick – provides a beautiful analogy. The fire at the tip of the wick of the evening lamp is supposed to be the Sun God himself.

9. As they blow conch in the jasmine blooms – As the jasmine bloom at dusk, the beetles gather. They make humming sound resembling the sound of a conch.

10. Tulsi – is a sacred plant in India. Its leaves are an integral part of rituals. It has medicinal properties as well. Generally, Tulsi will be planted on raised platforms to keep its purity.

10. THUS SPOKE THE GURU

This the debut day; and
You the novice actor,
Are bowing before me,
Touching my feet.
Everything will be alright,
Stride with confidence.
Your success brings glory
To both of us, alike.
Never forget that,
The melodious tunes and rhythms
Played in the background
Are not meant to entertain the actor
But to act as a tight rein on him.
You are the object to be seen;
The figure of an old era
With stunning attire and adornment,
Evoking curiosity
In the spectators you face.
Die, and enter
The body of the demigod
Whom you now embody
And move as it would.
As the curtain rises,
And you turn to face the bright light;

Even if it's the hundredth time,
A pain, a flutter in the stomach
An uneasiness, may sprout;
The only pleasure for an actor!
Discipline distilled acts as the
Liquor for transmogrification. *
As per me, this deft liquor
Bonds the actor to the stage.
In front of thousands watching,
How the facial expressions be
How controlled, free and elegant
The movements be
How the words are to be enacted;
Everything is pre-set for you;
So don't worry about it.
Nevertheless,
Unexpected things may happen.
Like expressions, movements
Or words from other artistes.
As the music reaches a crescendo,
If a mistake is committed by any
In movement or in a word!
Slipup may happen to anyone;
How deftly it is countered
Displays the adroitness of a person.
Whether it be on stage
Or in this vast world,
The dictum, in the nature of things
Is one and only one, my dear!

When you feel that,

Whatever you do may go wrong,

Then you need only to do resolutely,

What you intend to do!

Note: Transmogrification – The act or process of being transformed into a different form.

'Aasaan Paranjathu' - Published in Janayugam Onam special edition 1972.

Translated – May, 2023

Extracts from the long notes prepared by Shree K. P. Sankaran for this poem.

Guru-shishya (Master-Student) relation is very important in education and in art. In Kathakali, the renowned classical art form of Kerala, this relation is profound.

Guru, generally is considered as omniscient and Shishya, the incomplete human with all his limitations. The Guru and Shishya in this poem may well translate into God and man respectively. If so, what blessing and advice would God give to the man? This poem reveals a perspective by Edasseri, different from others.

After rigorous training, the shishya is now all set for his first performance and is in front of the Guru for his blessings. This poem is written in the form of advice from the great Guru; and lo! This is applicable to all in everyday life.

My Workshop - Edasseri

Mind has to traverse through a number of phases before any literary work takes shape. It is not possible to meticulously analyze the few initial phases of this process. During this phase my mind does not follow a rational path, but wanders through seemingly inscrutable and endless reveries. Something triggers a cause that makes mind tenderly emotional. The cause could be the elation from reading another book, an extraordinary personal experience or a memory that was awakened by a sound, a visual or a fragrance. There are many causal events that can transport one's mind into a state of introversion; any one of these is capable of acting as a trigger.

Mind has turned emotive and introvertive; will that state then develop into a poem? If so, how nice it would be! For, by now I would have produced my anthology of poems the size of ten "Mahabharathams". But a will has to operate at such times; an irresistible urge for writing a poem; for creation. Only then, the mind will emerge in an awakened state from the abyss of the unknown, bringing along the required 'ore' for the creation of a poem!

By the time such a stage for creation reaches, the mind must have traversed through many phases which do not have any definite contours or dividers. These phases can better be described as solitary dreams, rather than an intensive thought process of mind. Neither can it be portrayed, nor be termed as a purely conscious effort. I underline the word 'purely' because this does not happen in a situation void of thought and discretion. This is a phase full of irritations and anxieties turning one's mood rather nasty. It is a period that requires solitude more than ever. This period could be superficially construed as even non-productive due to its sheer inactivity. The significance of that period is that it happens in a time frame when the mind experiences undefined uneasiness lasting for days together and on looking back at a later date; long to have a repeat of that. I would like to call it as a sweet pain or an appealing agony. However, I have to mention that all these happen outside my work shop.

With the handful of 'ore' that my mind has dug up from the abyss of the unknown, I enter my work shop! Whatever be the turmoil, I am sure to mould something out of it. If I am to engage myself in a hundred issues outside - it happens - I will allot only that much attention as needed. My mind would always stay close to the melting malleable metal, like a mother would remain with her offspring notwithstanding the thousands of her household chores; all along trying to mold a shape out of it.

A brief explanation is needed here. Is it mere 'ore' that I have got with me? This metaphor actually falls short in front of the subjective evidence. While the "ore" I come up with is rather fluid and blurred and could be a mere subject, it could also be something amenable to my mind's rhythm and eager to be formed as a poem, often with two or three verses already formed, similar to the new leaves on a first sprout. May be what I got was an abstract image of a character, which would develop more clearly and which would get defined at the climax of a theme with lots of dramatic conflicts. In any case, it is the vision which is good enough to form a faint sense at least, with a 'beginning, middle and an end' of something that could be called as my creation later. There is, therefore, no meaning in calling it just 'ore'. Being a phenomenon , not clear enough in my imagination and which could involuntarily undergo transformations, to tell honestly, I myself am unable to name it.

I am trying to recollect the making of the narrative poem "The Fresh Claypot and the Scythe" (1948). There were two questions imprinted in my mind. Who sowed? Who reaped? The story of the poem does not have any significance other than being a plot that is able to powerfully connect these two questions. After spending a few days with the mind restless for unknown reasons and the same questions surging up high and rhyming repeatedly in my mind, the full poem was revealed with a beginning, middle and an end, as explained earlier.

'Who in the last season had sown,

The Aryan seeds in this field with love?'

After writing the above, it was not those lines as seen printed now in the book that were in my mind. They were the following lines, now seen in some other location.

'Who was it that reaped this year

The golden grain that Koman grew?'

Koman the farmer, the paddy field, his family, all were there in between these two separated verses.

This poem translated by Dr. Ayyappa Panicker, is provided below, for reference. In the original essay, the complete poem was not included. The forenote that Edasseri wrote for this poem is included.

'I have seen many a time, the legal attachment of crops and property like the animal sacrifice in temples. These unfortunate incidences are drastically coming down in numbers. Attachment of crops is one of the cruelties done legally with the help of 'court orders' and it may not be possible for the younger generations to believe it. I had close associations with all the three characters involved in this – The farmer, Land Lord and the Court. This poem is the result of such acquaintances.'

I.

Who in the last season had sown

The Aryan[1] seeds in this field with love?

When the hot sun of March burned

Rain-fire above, red embers below,

With his bullock waving its dewlap

Drawing the plough deep, unwearied;

Not with the sheen of oil glowed

His body, but with sweat;

Until the earth turned into fine dust,

Until Vishu[2] decked the Konna[3] with blossoms,

Koman had ploughed the field up and down;

Koman had sown the Aryan seeds.

When the clouds moved on leaving their print

On the field where fresh seeds sprouted,

Were there more golden shoots in the field

Or on the chest of Koman in rapture?

He had no rest either day or night,

What care he took to keep the watch!

The weeds too came up and grew thick

And the breeze thus blew to make music.

In the blue expanse all along

Swam and danced the water-waves,

Till the women flowed in like swans

To pluck and pick the weeds.

II.

The field did infest with weeds this year,

How hard for the farmer it was!

Gone is what was kept as seed corn;

Gone too what was meant for food!

Gone again the price of the bullock, sold,

Unmindful of the work after harvest!

Aromal Chekavar[4] won the joust,

Yet the weeds yielded not a span!

The bangles pleaded and flirted,

Yet the weeds yielded not a span!

Koman didn't pay his son's school fees,

Nor did he pay up his instalments,

And he didn't buy the prescription

For the fever his child caught from the new rains,

Gazing at her hands with the mylanchi[5] mark

Made long before the New Year's Eve,

The weed-picker girl started to cry;

What a wild game of the season's mischief!

III.

At the heel of the burning summer came

The all-upsetting thundershowers,

And as the rice seedlings overcome by thirst

Opened their sheaths to drink the rain water,

Koman too took the same clean drink;

That's of course what a father does.

And as the field grew dark and dense

With the spread of vacant spots,

When the dark rain had its orgy

Never stopping either night or day,

Till the ears of corn were seen

That brought sheer joy to the eye.

Koman was seen on the dyke

Like an oracle dancing his role.

When the first few torrential rains

In the last month of the year had ended,

There were the red-lipped ears of corn,

All along the level fields

With a heart given to ecstasy

Koman embraced his whole family.

What excitement in that house now,

To husk the paddy, to get fresh rice!

Father was fondling his little daughter

IV.

Seated on his knees; he coaxed her;

"A new skirt for my kitten

For the Onam[6] flower-festival."

Mother looked at the elder daughter,

Who seemed to pull a long face.

And father said, "If the yield is gold,

We'll spend it on a wedding locket."

"I didn't mean anything like that,"

The girl wearing glass bangles blushed.

"Three months' fees remain to be paid",

A hum arose somewhere in the group.

To each according to his desire;

The master of the house apportioned it.

Mother too had her private need;

"We must have pot to cook the new rice."

The soul of that family fluttered around

Like a dragonfly in that golden field;

And the ears grew heavy for a good harvest

Like a display of fireworks.

Are the dancers tired of the performance?

The rice plants lay down in full embrace.

As if to reap the moonlight of Onam

The golden sickle was rising.

People who passed by were heard to say;

"Koman has grown gold in this field."

V.

Who was it that reaped this year

The golden grain that Koman grew?

Neither Koman nor his men - but

A court officer and his henchmen!

The morning, they had fixed for the harvest

Gently opened her painted eyes.

The start of the celestial Arbor

Tossed about by the wild storm

Were slowly blossoming to grace

In the cluster of Tumpa flowers.

Koman came crossing the main dyke;

Behind him came his helpers.

Already the field was crowded;

The court officer got the harvest done.

Koman had just one glance of it;

All his desire was utterly lost;

As if he saw dogs barking

In the rice that was meant for a meal,

Koman had just one glance of it,

The power wielded by the court,

The revenge of the January crop

That withered for want of water from the sky,

This affront of attachment and harvest

For the rental arrears, the landlord's due?

VI.

The wrath of the reapers raised its hood

And began to blow and hiss.

Neeli, the Pulaya girl, fell on the ground

Beating her breast very hard.

"No one else shall reap this crop,"

Cheru Koman stepped down into the field.

Warming up to the fight and snarling

Like a leopard came forth Chathappan.

The hired harvesters cast away the sheaves

And quickly climbed the dykes.

Koman raged as if possessed,

Like an elephant chained to the post.

And that way came Koman's elder daughter,

A lovely little creeper,

Swinging and happy with the new pot

Bought to cook the new rice.

In her father's mind

Exploded a huge shell of fire,

She seemed like butter floating again

On the fire of his wrath.

In a few moments this treasure-land

Might turn into something strange.

On the dyke a voice arose to say

"Here are the orders; dare not disrespect them!"

Waving a piece of paper

There stood the court officer

Laying the land all barren

Like a rising cactus head!

VII.

Let the man who sowed see it;

The feudal order reaped the crop,

Sticking to the shade of the power;

A handful of robbers have kept all, for themselves.

The sickles lined up around the new pot

Which was of no use, any more,

The sickles useless for the harvest

Until sharpened against power; Pity!

The law leads the attack

On the land where the farmer grows the crop.

The results of that attack

Arise from the dyke,

The new pots and the sickles

Join and thunder on the dyke;

"First we must reap the real power;

Only after that, the Aryan crop!"

Their throats began to spread

This mantra in the heavens;

"First we must reap the real power;

Only after that, the Aryan crop!"

Notes: -

1. Aryan is a variety of rice.

2. Vishu a celebration, usually on the day the summer solstice starts.

3. Konna - A tree with bunches of yellow flowers, blossoms around March, April.

4.Aromal Chekavar was a hero of North Malabar in Kerala, whose adventurous duels were sung in eulogy by farm workers in Malabar.

5. Mylanchi - A floral decoration applied to the palm using the crushed leaves of Henna plant.

6. Onam - the harvest festival of Kerala lasting 10 days, when the courtyards are decorated with flowers.

Let me recollect yet another poem of mine. This poem is included in the anthology "Alakaavali".

Covert glances of mine alone,

Shall paint saffron, on blossom cheeks!

Breeze that bears your heart's fragrance,

No one else be able to breathe in.

No other eager ears get; a drop of this

Nectar of words, this flower rains.

If ever that kohl lined eyes take a look at,

Should that fall slyly on mine alone;

Whether for scribbling letters of love

Or for throwing angry looks!

(My sincerity. 1936)

It was only after writing these lines that I got complete picture of that poem. Then I went back and wrote the first stanza starting with "Let us go, let us go my darling, beyond the boundaries of the inquisitive world."

Have I ever written and published any poem just as it had sprouted in my mind? I don't remember. Chances are that I have not. I write continuously as if in a brain storming session, without proper form, structure or style and many portions remain raw since sufficient attention was not paid to finer details. Since many of my poems are narratives, I focus initially on the characters and scenes that are required to tell the story. The poems which are written continuously and therefore in a raw state will be subjected to critical examination before presenting to the general public, with those lines which were written in a flow further subjected to many intellectual changes like altering the shape of a few, transferring the positions of some or giving salvation yet to some others!

How much of critical approach is advisable in the course of creativity process? My experience says - not much! I remember instances when I had to totally discard creations with regret because of excessive self-criticism. That doesn't mean that there should not be any self-checking. As in many other instances, here also I follow a middle path.

It was a couple of my poet friends who prompted me to exercise some level of critical mind while writing poems. I remember them with gratitude. When we were young, we used to recite in our group the new poems written by us and to mercilessly criticize them. Immediately after writing "Premopaharangal" (Gifts of Love) I recited that poem in our group. They made me change many lines in that poem. Out of these I cannot forget those two lines written to narrate the ineptness of the hero to find out whether the expressions of the heroine were actually gestures of love or not and finally assuaging himself that she was like this before also. I must have changed it ten times at least, each change only intensifying their scorn and I on my part getting more and more infuriated out of embarrassment. We spent around two to three hours on that portion and dispersed. Adopting the stance of a laureate poet, I declared that those two lines are beyond correction. My friends passed the judgment that it would be embarrassingly bad if I leave it like that. After lunch when I was composed and returned to good mood, the apt lines came out involuntarily.

'Inscrutable was your face, earlier too

With the smile, those lovely lips

Never giving a hint,

Whether it begets fruit or not.'

Once again let me thank those terrible friends; they approved it! When the theme of poem is revealed in a rhymed manner, I like them naturally. Poems have a frame of mind that yearns for more fondness than any other genre of literature. Unless there is a severe grammatical mistake or a slight inappropriateness, I prefer not to change any verses. I will argue that, for the ever-growing language due to the constant interaction with other cultures, grammar has got only historical significance. But appropriateness is something that cannot be compromised.

I had searched my workshop several times, prior to writing this essay. Do the form and the content in a poem take birth simultaneously? The examples cited earlier do not give me a chance to doubt that it is not so. Not only that; no instance is coming to my mind, where I was looking for the form while keeping the content in mind or vice versa. Mind develops an abstract imagery. When that develops, the poem automatically gets evolved. This I can say from my experience, while acknowledging my ineptitude in poetics. I will also not proclaim that form evolves with a clear cut full blossomed imagery, like the content.

In the absence of admirers or friends, my Workshop now resembles a village black smith's workplace. With absolute dedication and concentration, I mould a penknife. With the slipping spectacles put back in position, I look at the penknife several times as if inspecting, but actually enjoying the beauty of it. There is a general saying that "even the best trained will not have sufficient self-confidence". So, turning towards the kitchen I call "Hey, please come here". My wife appears wiping out her hand in her clothes, as one who has undergone training on English cutleries. She will inspect my beautiful knife, examine it in and out and will return with an air of satisfaction and mostly with the comment, "What is there to doubt? Is this not how a cleaver looks like?"

Stooping, and without uttering a word I wipe it a couple of times more and give it to those who want it.

This was broadcast by All India Radio, Kozhikkode on 14.08.1962.

About The Author

Asokakumar Edasseri

Asokakumar Edasseri, son of the great poet Edasseri Govindan Nair, graduated in Mechanical Engineering from the Regional Engineering College, Calicut, (NIT). He retired from his professional career in 2016 from The Kingdom of Bahrain. After retirement he took an interest in literary activities. Asokakumar has translated several poems, short stories and essays. He can be contacted on mobile number (0091) 8281195300 or email asokedakkandy@gmail.com. He lives in Thrissur. "Janaki", 5A, Forus Cosy Nest, Machingal Lane, Thrissur - 680 001, Kerala, India.

www.ingramcontent.com/pod-product-compliance
Lightning Source LLC
Chambersburg PA
CBHW031306130726
47988CB00007B/2757